Texas Wineries

Wholly Revised 12th Printing

"Scattered throughout Texas, the wineries require a guide
for visitors to find them. Fortunately, this book
has done your legwork."
— Janet Wilson, *Austin American-Statesman*

By Barry Shlachter
& Amy Culbertson

Great Texas Line Press
Post Office Box 11105, Fort Worth, Texas 76110

Cover photo: Ralph Lauer
Book design: Ty Walls
Editor: Amy Culbertson
Printer: Hanson Printing, Fort Worth

Bulk sales of books from the Great Texas Line are available at special discounts for fund-raising, promotions and premiums.

Great Texas Line Press
Post Office Box 11105
Fort Worth, TX 76110
800-73TEXAS / Fax 817-926-0420
greattexas@hotmail.com

Visit our website to see the entire selection of Texas books:
www.greattexasline.com

Great Texas Line is a socially conscious publishing house, contracting with family-run firms to print its books while making every effort to engage writers, photographers, designers and editors who have had to leave daily journalism. It also donates a portion of proceeds from several books to Texas-based nonprofit groups, including Trinity Habitat for Humanity, North Fort Worth Historical Society, Texas Dance Hall Preservation and Big Bend Educational Foundation.

Table of Contents

Introduction 4

How to use this guide.. 5

Texas wine trails.. 6

Annual wine events 7-8

Winery listings
      Hill Country and Central Texas 9
      Panhandle Plains and West Texas 58
      North Central Texas 68
      Northeast Texas 91
      Southeast Texas.. 104

Texas wine and food pairings 118

Alphabetical index of wineries 119-120

Introduction

What could be finer than sitting on an oak-shaded patio, sipping a refreshingly crisp white wine or a full-bodied red — made just a few feet away?

Now factor in a leisurely tour of the vineyards and grounds, a tête-à-tête with the winemaker about his wine's distinctively Lone Star terroir and maybe some sightseeing, shopping and barbecue along the way.

Yes, wine tourism is big business in Texas. Wineries can be found in most corners of the state, and new ones are opening regularly — often with calendars of events and amenities from gourmet meals to live music. The Hill Country is taking pages from Napa Valley's book, even drawing wineries from other regions to open tasting rooms there.

The "Chateau Bubba" stigma is definitely receding for Texas winemakers. Most observers agree that recent years have seen massive advances in the overall quality of wines made in Texas; with the locavore movement gaining momentum, it's never been hipper for Texans to seek out Texas wines.

Not only is the state's wine scene getting better; it's becoming more diverse. Texas winemakers are thinking outside the box, adventurously planting and blending all manner of not-so-well-known European and native American grapes to see what works in their particular soil and climate. And most wineries offer a roster of wine styles to suit widely varying tastes, whether for sophisticated and complex bottles or for fun, fruity and sweet ones.

Today, you'll find eight recognized appellations, or American viticultural areas, in Texas. Most of the state's major cities boast wineries within easy driving distance, and there are plenty of out-of-the-way finds for wine trippers who enjoy the charms of farm-to-market roads.

With this little volume, you can identify places to stop for a sip wherever in Texas you may roam.

Barry Shlachter
Amy Culbertson
Fort Worth

How to Use the Guide

The only thing a venture needs to call itself a winery legally in Texas is a single piece of winemaking equipment. It doesn't even have to make wine. In this book, though, we've restricted our listings to places we consider true wineries, those producing wines with a real Texas connection and those that welcome visitors. Off-site tasting rooms are generally listed with the original winery, not as separate entries.

You can keep our guide in your car or purse, to pull out for spontaneous stops during day trips, or use it to plot out a wine-centric weekend or a longer vacation. Each listing offers info on the winery's hours and its wines, contact information, maps with directions and intelligence on visitor amenities.

As the map shows, we've organized the book by regions: Hill Country and Central Texas, Panhandle Plains and West Texas, North Central Texas, Northeast Texas and Southeast Texas. Wineries are listed alphabetically in each region, with a statewide alphabetical index at the book's end.

To help you round out your itinerary, we've ferreted out things to see or do in the vicinity of many of the wineries, as well as dining and lodging options if you're seeking something beyond a Golden Corral or Days Inn (see "Worth stopping for" and "Overnighting" sections after individual listings).

Note that winery hours can change seasonally, or at the owner's whim or need. Websites are not always updated religiously, either. If in doubt, call ahead.

We've done our best to offer the most comprehensive listings and up-to-date information, so let us know if we've overlooked anything: greattexas@hotmail.com.

Texas Wine Trails

All over Texas, wineries have banded together to create wine trails to help promote their products. At last count, we found more than a dozen such trails, and they are organizing so prolifically that there could be more by the time you read this. Each trail represents several wineries in a specific region or along a particular byway; each hosts annual seasonal events. See each trail's website for its member wineries.

Cross Timbers Wine Trail, North Central Texas, www.crosstimberswinetrail.com.

Dallas Wine Trail, city of Dallas, www.dallaswinetrail.com.

Fredericksburg Wine Road 290, in Fredericksburg and along U.S. 290 in the Hill Country, www.wineroad290.com.

Grapevine Wine Trail, city of Grapevine in North Central Texas, www.grapevinewinetrail.com.

Guadalupe Valley Wine Trail, Comfort-Sisterdale area of the Hill Country, www.guadalupevalleywinetrail.com.

Munson Wine Trail, North Central Texas, www.munsonwinetrail.com.

Piney Woods Wine Trail, Northeast Texas, www.pineywoodswinetrail.com.

Red River Wine Trail, along U.S. 82 in North Central Texas, www.redriverwinetrail.com.

San Gabriel Wine Trail, Interstate 35 corridor north of Austin, www.sangabrielwinetrail.com.

Texas Bluebonnet Wine Trail, Southeast Texas, www.texasbluebonnetwinetrail.com.

Texas High Plains Wine & Vine Trail, West Texas' Lubbock area, www.highplainswinetrail.com.

Texas Hill Country Wineries, www.texaswinetrail.com.

Top of the Hill Country Wine Trail, northernmost section of the Hill Country, northwest of Austin, www.topofhillcountrycom.

Way Out Wineries, between Fort Worth and the northern Hill Country, bridging North Central and Central Texas, www.wayoutwineries.org.

Annual Wine Events

New wine events are popping up all the time, all over Texas. Here's a list of some of the more established annual wine celebrations.

January
• Port 'n' Pairings, Fredericksburg Wine Road 290 wineries, www.wineroad290.com
• Winter Wine Trail, San Gabriel Wine Trail wineries, www.sangabrielwinetrail.com
• White (and Reds) Sale, Way Out Wineries, www.wayoutwineries.org
• San Antonio Wine Competition, www.sawinefest.com

February
• Wine & Chocolate Trail, Texas Bluebonnet Wine Trail wineries, www.texasbluebonnetwinetrail.com
• Ragin' Cajun, Fredericksburg Wine Road 290 wineries, www.wineroad290.com
• San Antonio Wine Festival, www.sawinefest.com
• Wine Lovers Trail, Texas Hill Country Wineries, www.texaswinetrail.com
• Mardi Gras Road Trip, Way Out Wineries, www.wayoutwineries.org
• The Dallas Morning News and Texsom Wine Competition, Dallas, www.dallaswinecomp.com

February-March
• Houston Livestock Show and Rodeo "Rodeo Uncorked!" Wine Show, www.rodeohouston.com/events/wine/index.aspx

March
• Savor Dallas, www.savordallas.com
• SpringFest Wine and Art Festival, Old Town Spring, www.winefestoldtownspring.com
• Vino and Pasta, Fredericksburg Wine Road 290, www.wineroad290.com
• Denison Arts and Wine Renaissance, www.denisonartsculture.com

April
• Texas Hill Country Wine and Food Festival, Austin, www.texaswineandfood.org
• Castroville Area Chamber of Commerce Wine & Beer Fest, Castroville, www.castroville.com
• Blessing of the Vines and New Vintage Wine & Gallery Trail, Grapevine, www.grapevinetexasusa.com
• Wine & Wildflowers Trail, Texas Hill Country Wineries, www.texaswinetrail.com
• Wildflower Road Trip, Way Out Wineries, www.wayoutwineries.org
• New Vintage Wine & Art Festival, Grapevine, www.grapevinetexasusa.com
• Galveston Island Food & Wine Festival, Galveston, www.galveston.com/foodandwine
• San Angelo Wine and Food Festival, www.sanangeloarts.com
• Spring Bluebonnet Wine & Cheese Trail, Texas Bluebonnet Wine Trail, www.texasbluebonnetwinetrail.com
• Wine and Roses Festival, Bryan
• Dallas Wine and Food Festival, www.dallaswineandfoodfestival.com
• The Grand Wine & Food Affair, Sugar Land, www.thegrandwineandfoodaffair.com

May
• Culinaria Wine & Culinary Arts Festival, San Antonio, www.culinariasa.com
• Piney Woods Wine Festival, Mt. Vernon, www.pineywoodswinetrail.com
• Rockport Festival of Wine and Food, www.texasfestivalofwines.com

June
• Lone Star International Wine Competition, Grapevine, www.txwines.org/competitions/lonestar.asp

- Summertime Cook-Off Road Trip, Way Out Wineries, www.wayoutwineries.org
- Vino el Pastor, Fredericksburg Wine Road 290 wineries, www.wineroad290.com

July
- Taste of the Hill Country, Burnet, www.tasteofthehillcountrytx.com/
- Trivial Pursuit, Cross Timbers Wine Trail, www.crosstimberswinetrail.com
- Picnic Road Trip, Way Out Wineries, www.wayoutwineries.org
- GO TEXAN Restaurant Round-Up, www.gotexanrestaurantroundup.com
- Harvest Trail, Texas Bluebonnet Wine Trail, www.texasbluebonnetwinetrail.com

August
- Harvest Wine Trail, Texas Hill Country wineries, www.texaswinetrail.com

September
- GrapeFest, Grapevine, www.grapevinetexasusa.com
- Houston Wine Fest, www.houstonwinefest.com
- Dripping With Taste Wine & Food Festival, Dripping Springs, www.drippingwithtaste.org

- Tailgate Road Trip, Way Out Wineries, www.wayoutwineries.org
- Kiolbassa and Kabernet, Fredericksburg Wine Road 290 wineries, www.wineroad290.com
- Montgomery Wine Fest, Montgomery, www.historicmontgomerytexas.com

October
- Texas Wine Month, www.gotexanwine.org
- Texas Wine Month Trail, Texas Hill Country Wineries, www.texaswinetrail.com
- October Wine & Sausage Trail, Texas Bluebonnet Wine Trail wineries, www.texasbluebonnetwinetrail.com
- Lubbock Wine Festival, www.lubbockwinefestival.com
- San Saba River Pecan Jam, San Saba, www.pecanjam.com
- Gruene Music and Wine Festival, Gruene, www.gruenemusicandwinefest.org
- Lampasas Wine Tour, Lampasas, www.lampasaschamber.org/7900545_47902.htm
- Texas Reds Steak & Grape Festival, Bryan, www.texasredsfestival.com

- La Dolce Vita Food and Wine Festival, Austin, www.amoa.org
- Fredericksburg Food & Wine Fest, www.fbgfoodandwinefest.com
- Wicked Wine Trail, Red River Wine Trail wineries, www.redriverwinetrail.com

November
- Houston Livestock Show and Rodeo International Wine Competition, www.rodeohouston.com/events/wine/international.aspx
- Texas Fall Fest & Wine Auction, Horseshoe Bay/Marble Falls, www.texasfallfest.com

December
- Holiday Road Trip, Way Out Wineries, www.wayoutwineries.org
- Edible Austin Eat Drink Local Week, Austin
- Holiday Wine & Crystal Trail, Texas Bluebonnet Wine Trail wineries, www.texasbluebonnetwinetrail.com
- Holiday Wine Trail, Texas Hill Country Wineries, www.texaswinetrail.com
- Christmas Experience, Red River Wine Trail, www.redriverwinetrail.com

For this year's dates and details, check the individual websites or www.gotexanwine.org, or call 866-4TXWINE.

The Wineries
Hill Country and Central Texas

From its northern fringes up in San Saba County to south of San Antonio, the Hill Country is the heart of wine traveling in Texas.

We've heard it described as the Napa Valley of Texas. While the comparison may be overreaching just a tad, we get the point: Central Texas combines some of Texas' most appealing countryside with the state's heaviest concentration of wineries, many of them producing praiseworthy bottles. A few years back, the Orbitz.com travel website ranked the Texas Hill Country the second-fastest-growing wine destination in the U.S., behind Napa, of course.

With its picturesque outcrops and rivers, lakes and live oaks, its barbecue and bluebonnets and its German pioneer heritage, the Hill Country has long been a beloved Texas road-trip destination. Wine entered the picture back in the '70s, when Ed and Susan Auler of Fall Creek Winery started planting grapes near Lake Buchanan; other wine trailblazers soon followed suit. In the early '90s, Dr. Richard Becker established Becker Vineyards, whose wines would become some of the state's best-known. A few years later, pioneers like Becker alumnus Jim Johnson and his wife Karen, at Alamosa Wine Cellars, and Rick and Madelyn Naber, at Flat Creek Estate, began planting warm-climate varietals, marking a new chapter in Texas winemaking.

Today, Central Texas is home to upwards of 50 wineries and counting. New blood in the form of wineries such as Perissos, Bending Branch, Duchman and William Chris is bringing Texas winemaking forward into the 21st century with adventurous grape varietals.

And now we're seeing winemakers from other regions of Texas colonizing the Hill Country. An unprecedented wine boom has seen three new tasting rooms open on a scant quarter-mile of U.S. 290 just east of Fredericksburg: a joint venture, 4.0 Cellars, by the triumvirate of Kim McPherson of Lubbock's McPherson Cellars, Pat Brennan of Comanche's Brennan Vineyards and Gene Estes of Burleson's Lone Oak; an elaborate outpost of Southeast Texas' Messina Hof; and Mendelbaum Cellars, showcasing wines from Dan Gatlin's Inwood Estates in Dallas and the Vineyard at Florence.

Alamosa Wine Cellars

Bend and Lampasas.

Bend winery: 3 miles west of Bend off FM 580.
677 County Road 430, Bend • 325-628-3313
www.alamosawinecellars.com • wine@alamosawinecellars.com
Tastings, tours: Sat. 10 a.m.-5 p.m., (on special-event days such as wine-trail tours, open Fri.-Sat. 10 a.m.-6 p.m., Sun. noon-5 p.m.). Tastings free.

Lampasas tasting room: On U.S. 281 a mile south of the intersection of U.S. 190 and U.S. 183. 2204 U.S. 281, Lampasas • 512-556-0001
Tastings, tours: Mon.-Wed. 11 a.m.-6 p.m., Thu.-Sat. 11 a.m.-7 p.m., Sun. noon-5 p.m. (closing hours may vary, so call ahead).
Varieties: Orange Muscat, Syrah, Tempranillo, Viognier; Texas port; red and white blends using Cinsault, Graciano, Grenache, Mourvèdre, Roussanne, Sangiovese, Syrah, Tempranillo, Verdello and Viognier grapes.

Sitting just west of Bend – near a horseshoe bend in the Colorado River, between San Saba and Lampasas – this winery draws its grapes from its 10-acre vineyard and from like-minded Texas growers.

Owner and winemaker Jim Johnson, a graduate of UC Davis' famed oenology program with several major California wineries on his resumé, also had winemaking stints with a couple of respected Texas wineries under his belt before opening his own place.

Alamosa was among the pioneering Texas wineries to concentrate on warm-climate varietals — especially Rhone grapes, which thrive in the hot, dry conditions of the northern Hill Country. Johnson discovered that the grapes that produce Spain's Rioja wines are grown in limestone-rich soil similar to that in the northern edge of the Llano uplift. He and his wife Karen used the Spanish Tempranillo grape to produce a horned-frog-labeled wine known as El Guapo, which gained quite a following for Alamosa — and not just among TCU partisans.

The Johnsons' self-described "little pissant winery" is committed to using 100 percent Texas grapes. Johnson doesn't believe in entering wine competitions, but he's garnered plenty of acclaim without them. The seventh edition of Robert Parker's "Parker's Wine Buying Guide" lists Alamosa among only six wineries in Texas as being worth special note.

The Bend tasting room sells gifts and gourmet foods as well as wine, and

Alamosa is part of three wine trails: the Way Out Wineries wine trail, the Texas Hill Country Wineries trail and the Top of the Hill Country Wine Trail.

The Johnsons' latest addition, an Alamosa tasting room in nearby Lampasas, features a wine bar, frozen margaritas and sangrias and a gift shop, and it's open seven days a week.

Worth stopping for: Colorado Bend State Park (Bend), popular for fishing and camping, offers cave tours and tours of the 60-foot Gorman Falls (915-628-3240, http://www.tpwd.state. tx.us/spdest/findadest/parks/colorado_bend/). **Bad Bob's Bend Store** (Bend) sells burgers, bait and sundries (325-628-3523). **Regency Suspension Bridge**, spanning the Colorado River in Regency, between San Saba and Brownwood, is much photographed. In Lampasas, **Hancock Springs Free Flow Pool**, built in 1911 and fed by one of the sulphur springs that made Lampasas a spa destination in its early years, is still open in summer (512-556-6031). **Storm's Drive-In** (Lampasas) is a classic 1950-vintage burger stand and the original in a Hill Country mini-chain (512-556-6269, www.stormsrestaurants.com).

Becker Vineyards

11 miles east of Fredericksburg and 3 miles west of Stonewall, off U.S. 290. Exit Jenschke Lane; turn right at 464 Becker Farms Road.

464 Becker Farms Road, Stonewall
830-644-2681 • www.beckervineyards.com
beckervyds@beecreek.net

Tastings, tours: Mon.-Thu. 10 a.m.-5 p.m., Fri.-Sat. 10 a.m.-6 p.m., Sun. noon-6 p.m. Closed on major holidays. Tasting fee.
Varieties: Barbera, Cabernet Franc, Cabernet Sauvignon, Chardonnay, Chenin Blanc, Fumé Blanc, Gewürztraminer, Grenache, Malbec, Muscat Canelli, Pinot Grigio, Syrah and a Syrah-based port-style fortified wine, Riesling, Viognier, Zinfandel; red blends using Carignane, Cabernet Franc, Cabernet Sauvignon, Grenache, Malbec, Merlot, Mourvèdre, Petit Verdot and Syrah.

Surrounded by Fredericksburg's famous peach orchards, pastures holding grazing quarter horses and fields of Provençal lavender stands Becker's 10,000-square-foot winery, built in the fashion of a 19th-century German stone barn. Adjacent is a log cabin, circa 1880, which serves as the Homestead Bed and Breakfast, a popular honeymoon retreat, where a bottle of Becker wine comes with your room.

Dr. Richard and Bunny Becker established their first vineyards in 1992, with the first commercial harvest three years later. They expanded their operations in 1997 with the purchase of the Bluebonnet Hill Vineyard in Ballinger. The enterprising couple planted three acres of lavender behind their main vineyard in 1998 for commercial sale, and in 2001 they added 10 acres to their front vineyards, for a total of 46 acres. The vines are drip-irrigated with water drawn from limestone formations 300 feet beneath the surface. The estate boasts the largest underground wine cellar in Texas, where each vintage matures in French and American oak barrels.

Most of its wines are well-respected, but Becker may be most celebrated for its reserve Cabs and its Viogniers (it makes a late-harvest Viognier too). Wine pooh-bah Robert Parker mentions Becker among only six Texas wineries of note in his seventh edition of "Parker's Wine Buyer's Guide."

As one of the most popular Hill Country wine destinations, Becker's tasting room — boasting a large stone fireplace and the original bar from San Antonio's 19th-century Green Tree Saloon — is frequently packed despite its size. In 2003 the Beckers opened the Lavender Haus reception hall for private events and wine dinners. There's a covered veranda, too.

Becker is the most prominent of the nine wineries on the Fredericksburg Wine Road 290 wine trail and a member of the Texas Hill Country Wineries, as well. The Beckers host a Lavender Festival each spring.

Visitors are welcome to use the picnic facilities, browse in the gift shop or check out the wine and cheese display case; a reception hall hosts special events. In December 2008, *Bon Appétit* magazine named Becker Vineyards one of its favorite "off-the-beaten-path" wineries.

Worth stopping for: Fredericksburg makes much of its **German pioneer heritage** with a slew of historic buildings and museums (888-997-3600, www.visitfredericksburgtx.org). Home to the stunning six-acre **National Museum of the Pacific War** complex (www.nimitz-museum.org), downtown Fredericksburg is chockablock with shops such as **Der Kuchen Laden** kitchen store (830-997-4937, www.littlechef.com); wine bars; and sweet little eateries such as **Rather Sweet Bakery & Café** (830-990-0498, www.rathersweet.com), **Peach Tree Tea Room** (830-997-9527, www.peach-tree.com) and **Fromage du Monde** (830-992-3134, www.fromagedumonde.com). Just east of the city on U.S. 290 is a growing wine complex that includes, along with the established Grape Creek Vineyards, three new tasting rooms: the much-buzzed-about **4.0 Cellars** (see page 26); **Mendelbaum Cellars** (see page 34); and **Messina Hof Hill Country** (830-990-4653, www.messinahof.com/mhhillcountry), an ambitious offshoot of the Bryan wine theme park, set on a Teutonic 10-acre compound complete with B&B cottages (see page 109). Ten miles west of the city, on U.S. 87, lies the **Hill Top Café**, serving Cajun-Greek eats in a quirky Texas honky-tonk setting (830-997-8922, www.hilltopcafe.com). Too much wine? Try **Fredericksburg Brewing Com-**

pany, an award-winning brewpub with a B&B upstairs, at 245 E. Main downtown (830-997-1646). The 21st-century theme-park incarnation of the **Fredericksburg Herb Farm** has a restaurant, spa and several "Sunday house" B&B cottages (830-997-8615, www.fredericksburgherbfarm. com), while fans of the original herb farm will find handmade herbal products from the original owner at his **URBANherbal** shop (830-456-9667, www.urbanherbal.com). Nature lovers have plenty of options, starting with the **Live Oak Wilderness Nature Trail** in Lady Bird Johnson **Municipal Park** (http://www.fbgtx.org/departments/ladybirdpark.htm). Ten miles south of Fredericksburg on Old San Antonio Road is the **Old Tunnel Wildlife Management Area**, where from mid-May to mid-October millions of Mexican free-tail bats emerge from a long-abandoned railway tunnel (866-978-2287, http://www.tpwd.state.tx.us/huntwild/hunt/wma/find_a_wma/list/?id=17). **Pedernales Falls State Park**, in Blanco County east of Johnson City, hosts camping, picnicking, hiking, swimming, tubing, mountain biking and fishing (830-868-7304, http://www.tpwd.state. tx.us/spdest/findadest/parks/pedernales_falls/). The nearby Hill Country towns of **Luckenbach, Johnson City, Stonewall** and **Blanco** offer attractions such as the **Lyndon B. Johnson National Historical Park**, which actually comprises two parks, one in Johnson City, with a visitor center and Johnson's boyhood home, and the LBJ Ranch near Stonewall (830-868-7128, www. nps.gov/lyjo).

Overnighting: Fredericksburg and environs probably boast more inns, B&Bs, cottages and hotels per acre than any other town in Texas. One of the largest B&B reservation services is **Gastehaus Schmidt** (866-427-8374, www.fbglodging.com), which offers scores of lodging choices, from B&Bs to guesthouses to private homes in or out of town. Looking for something different? You can park your plane in front of your room at the **Hangar Hotel**, a themed boutique-style hotel and diner built to resemble a World War II hangar, overlooking the Gillespie County Airport (830-997-9990) just outside town. In Stonewall, **Rose Hill Manor**, a replica of an Old South plantation house, has four suites, a reputation for fine dining and a view of the Pedernales River Valley (830-644-2247, www.rose-hill.com). Over in Johnson City, the stately **Chantilly Lace Country Inn Bed & Breakfast** in Johnson City offers six acres of gardens, a lavender field, verandas, porches and a restaurant open to the public for weekend dinners (830-660-2621 or 830-637-9080, www. chantillylacesoaps.com).

Bell Mountain Vineyards

14 miles north of Fredericksburg off Texas 16.

463 Bell Mountain Road, Fredericksburg
830-685-3297 • www.bellmountainwine.com
contactus@bellmountainwine.com

Winery: Sat. 10 a.m.-5 p.m. from the first Saturday of February through the last Saturday in December; by appointment other days except Sun.; call at least 24 hours in advance.

Fredericksburg tasting rooms: Oberhof Wine Cellars, in Das Peach Haus, 1 1/2 miles south of Fredericksburg's Main Street at 1406 S. U.S. 87, Mon.-Sat. 10 a.m.-6 p.m., Sun. noon-6 p.m.
BMV Tasting, next to Der Kuchen Laden at 256 E. Main St., Mon.-Fri. noon-5:30 p.m., Sat. 10 a.m.-6 p.m., Sun. noon-4 p.m.
Varieties: Estate-bottled Cabernet Sauvignon (and a rosé of Cabernet), Chardonnay, Merlot, Pinot Noir, Riesling (dry and late-harvest) and blends; fruit wines and mead.

On the slopes of Bell Mountain, in an area designated in 1986 as Texas' first wine-growing area by the federal government, the vineyard is planted on 56 acres of sandy-loam soils, replete with rich minerals and blessed with a moderate climate due to its elevation.

Aside from varietal wines under the Bell Mountain label, Bob and Evelyn Oberhelman also produce a spiced red wine, a raspberry wine, a peach-infused rosé wine and mead fermented from Texas wildflower honey under the Oberhof Wine label.

The operation includes a wine and gourmet food shop; check the winery's website for year-round events.

Bell Mountain's wines can be tasted at two Fredericksburg tasting rooms, Oberhof Wine Cellars inside Das Peach Haus and BMV Tasting next to Der Kuchen Laden.

Worth stopping for/overnighting: See **Becker Vineyards** listing, page 11.

Bella Vista Cellars

On Bella Vista Ranch 5 miles north of Wimberley. From Wimberley Square, go north on Ranch Road 12, left on Jacob's Well Road for 1.6 miles, right on Mount Sharp Road for 2 miles to the ranch gate.

3101 Mount Sharp Road, Wimberley • 512-847-6514
www.texasoliveoil.com • oliveguy@bvranch.com

Tastings, tours: Thu.-Sat. 10 a.m.-5 p.m., Sun. noon-4 p.m.; tours at 10 a.m. and 1 p.m. Sat. and noon Sun.; group tours by appointment Mon.-Wed. Tasting/tour fees.
Varieties: Cabernet Franc, Cabernet Sauvignon, Chenin Blanc, Syrah, Sangiovese; blackberry and blueberry.

Bella Vista is not just a boutique winery a few miles from the quaint Hill Country community of Wimberley. The idea was to create a traditional Italian family farm, a "touch of Tuscany" in the middle of the Lone Star state, with a producing olive orchard, frantoio (olive press), vineyard, winery, balsamic vinegars, preserves — and, of course, handcrafted wines. The jams are made from the ranch's own raspberries, blackberries and figs.

First Texas Olive Oil is made on site and is, of course, available for sale at the ranch's retail store or for tasting in the tasting room. You can buy olive trees at Bella Vista as well.

Tour the olive orchard and gardens, olive press and winery and finish with a guided tasting of olive oils and wines during the weekend.

Worth stopping for: The quaintsy-posh Hill Country town of **Wimberley** (www.wimberley.org) teems with boutiques, craft galleries, gift shops and eateries, including the **Leaning Pear** (512) 847-7327, www.leaningpear.com), a contemporary café with both traditional and innovative fare. You can grab a cupcake and an iced tea at the pink-and-blue **How Sweet It Is** stand on the square (512-922-6661), an outpost of the **Sugar Shack Bakery** on Ranch Road 12 (512-847-0477). From March through December, antiquers and flea-market aficionados flock to Wimberley for outdoor **Market Days** (www.shopmarketdays.com) on the first Saturday of each month. Driftwood's **Salt Lick BBQ**, across the road from the Civil-War-era **Camp Ben McCulloch**, is one of Texas' better-known 'cue joints (512-894-3117, www.saltlickbbq.com).
Overnighting: The highly lauded **Blair House Inn** in Wimberley (512-847-1111 or 877-549-5450, www.blairhouseinn.com) sets the standard for B&Bs in the area, with lavishly furnished rooms and cottages, a spa and pool, a respected cooking school and Saturday dinners (open to the public; reservations required).

Bell Springs Winery

Just north of Dripping Springs, 3 miles north of U.S. 290.

3700 Bell Springs Road, Dripping Springs
830-483-9463 • www.bellspringswinery.com

Tastings, tours: Thu. noon-5 p.m., Fri. noon-6 p.m., Sat.-Sun. 11 a.m.-6 p.m. Tasting and tour fees.
Varieties: Cabernet Franc, Chardonnay, Malvasia Bianca, Merlot, Nebbiolo, Pinot Grigio, Sangiovese, Sauvignon Blanc, Syrah, Trebbiano, Viognier, Zinfandel; blends and dessert wine.

Just outside Dripping Springs lies this laid-back winery established in 2009. Its modest winery and tasting room — new construction but with a "Texas red barn" look — sits amid oak and cedar. Don't expect a vineyard, though — Bell Springs doesn't grow its own grapes or even use Texas grapes; it buys its grapes from California and other regions.

There's a covered deck and concrete patio as well as lots of space for picnicking under those trees. Cheese plates are available in the tasting room, but feel free to bring your own food, as well as blankets or lawn chairs for lounging or sitting.

Expect frequent live music and other special events from cookouts to car shows (check the website; it's also on the Texas Hill Country Wineries trail. No kids under 16 are admitted, but leashed and well-behaved dogs are fine; the owners' two dogs have the run of the place.

Worth stopping for: North of Dripping Springs, **Hamilton Pool Preserve**, a grotto-like natural pool crowned by a 50-foot waterfall, is a popular destination from Austin (call ahead for swimming conditions, 512-264-2740, www.co.travis.tx.us/tnr/parks/hamilton_pool.asp). Dripping Springs' proximity to Austin means a number of dining options that are a cut above the usual, including **Creek Road Café** (512-858-9459, www.creekroadcafe.com), the **Goodnight Diner** (512-858-0426, thegoodnightdiner.org and the little **Thyme and Dough bakery** (512-894-0001, www. thymeanddough.com). **Lyndon B. Johnson National Historical Park** comprises two parks, one in Johnson City, with a visitor center, Johnson's boyhood home and the Johnson Settlement, and the LBJ Ranch 14 miles west of Johnson City near Stonewall (830-868-7128, www.nps.gov/lyjo). Several **lavender farms** can be found near Johnson City; check http://www.johnsoncitytexaschamber.com/things_to_do/index.html.**Pedernales Falls State Park**, in Blanco County east of Johnson City, offers camping, picnicking, hiking, river swimming, tubing, wading, mountain biking, fishing, bird-watching (830-868-7304). **Bella Vista Ranch** (between Driftwood and Wimberley) is planted with more than 1,000 olive trees (512-842-1240, www.texasoliveoil.com). Driftwood's **Salt Lick BBQ**, across the road from the Civil-War-era Camp Ben McCulloch, is one of Texas' better-known 'cue joints (512-894-3117, www.saltlickbbq.com).

Overnighting: Nearby **Juniper Hills Farm** (830-833-0910, www.juniperhillsfarm.com) offers upscale cabins, cooking classes, massages and other indulgences. The highly lauded **Blair House Inn** in Wimberley (512-847-1111 or 877-549-5450, www.blairhouseinn.com) sets the standard for B&Bs in the area, with lavishly furnished rooms and cottages, a spa and pool, a respected cooking school and Saturday dinners (open to the public; reservations required).

Bending Branch Winery

From Interstate 10, go north on U.S. 87, west on Texas 27, south on Hermann Sons Road, then east on Lindner Branch Trail.

142 Lindner Branch Trail, Comfort • 830-995-2948
bendingbranchwinery.com • jen@bendingbranchwinery.com

Tastings, tours: Fri.-Sat. 11 a.m.-6 p.m., Sun. noon-5 p.m. and by appointment. Fee.

Varieties: Cabernet Sauvignon, Petite Sirah, Picpoul Blanc, Tannat.

Hill Country and Central Texas

This winery on 56 scenic acres works to be green. The two-generation family venture follows sustainable practices to produce organically made wines.

Bending Branch's signature grape is Tannat, long associated with the Madiran region of southwest France, where it is known for its high tannins. A softer variety has thrived in the New World.

Robert Young, a doctor who moved from Atlanta to follow his dream of creating a winery, transforms the Tannat grape "into a thick, near-black wine that's bold in flavor and hardy by its Pyrenees-to-Texas lineage," wrote wine judge and blogger Russ Kane.

"Bob summed it up best when he said, 'Tannat's just a natural for the Lone Star State. It just seems to want to grow here. We think that this will be a superstar, used both for single-varietal wines and also in blends with other red grapes,'" Kane quoted Young.

Young is just ramping up commercial production from his own 13 acres of vines; he started out with grapes purchased from High Plains growers and from California. Early on, he won awards for his Petite Sirah, Picpoul Blanc, Souzão and Tannat.

Bending Branch participates in events on the Texas Hill Country Wineries and Guadalupe Valley wine trails. Check out the winery website for other events.

Worth stopping for: Comfort has what is believed to be Texas' only Civil War memorial to the Union cause – **Treue der Union Monument** – at the graves of a group of settlers dedicated to the Union, which many in the old German community supported. The settlers were killed by Confederate soldiers as they were fleeing Texas for Mexico. The monument is on the west side of Comfort, 1½ blocks north of Texas 27 on High Street. About 13 miles north of Comfort is the **Old Tunnel Wildlife Management Area**, where from mid-May to mid-October millions of Mexican free-tail bats emerge from a long-abandoned railway tunnel (866-978-2287, http://www.tpwd.state.tx.us/huntwild/hunt/wma/find_a_wma/list/?id=17). Hidden away in the barely-there hamlet of Welfare, **Welfare Café** is a one-of-a-kind restaurant whose food and setting will amaze you (Wed.-Sun., 830-537-3700, www.welfarecafe.net).

Overnighting: At **Meyer Bed and Breakfast** on Cypress Creek, six buildings, including an 1857 stagecoach stop, have been made into an inn with a pool, hot tub, fireplaces in most rooms and a nature area on the edge of Comfort (888-995-6100, www.meyerbedandbreakfast.com). Just southwest of Comfort, **Riven Rock Ranch** is an ambitious enclave of handsome period-style buildings on a working farm overlooking the Guadalupe River. It offers rooms and cottages; a pool and native garden; and a restaurant providing breakfast to guests and lunch and dinner Fri.-Sun. There's also a vineyard with plans for a future winery (830-995-4045, www.rivenrockranch.com). **Ye Kendall Inn** in Boerne houses antiques-filled guest rooms done to the nines and cooks up great chops and more in a pre-Civil-War-era stone inn (800-364-2138, www.yekendallinn.com).

Brennan Vineyards

See listing in **"North Central"** section, page 72

Chisholm Trail Winery

9 miles west of Fredericksburg, on Usener Road 2 1/2 miles south of U.S. 290.

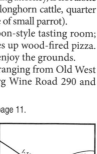

2367 Usener Road, Fredericksburg
830-990-2675 • 877-990-CORK (2675)
www.chisholmtrailwinery.com • chisholmtrail@beecreek.net

Tastings, tours: Noon-6 p.m. daily (except major holidays); tours by appointment. Tasting fee.
Varieties: Blanc du Bois, Lenoir (Black Spanish), a sweet white Merlot and both sweet and dry blends, including Jackass Blush.

West of Fredericksburg, near pastures dotted with Texas longhorn cattle and wildflowers, this cattle-drive-themed winery began production in 1999 and opened to the public in 2001.

Owner and winemaker Paula K. Williamson, a recovering attorney, is not alone at the 23-acre vineyard on her 80-acre ranch. There are longhorn cattle, quarter horses, a pot-bellied pig and a peach-faced conure (a type of small parrot).

Visitors can get into the Old West spirit in the saloon-style tasting room; on weekends, the winery's Oval Oven restaurant serves up wood-fired pizza. Outside, picnickers can settle down by the creek and enjoy the grounds.

See the winery website for frequent winery events, ranging from Old West shootouts to formal dinners, including Fredericksburg Wine Road 290 and Texas Hill Country Wineries themed events.

Worth stopping for/overnighting: See **Becker Vineyards** listing, page 11.

Comfort Cellars Winery

Downtown Comfort.

723 Front St. (Texas 27), Comfort • 830-995-3274
www.comfortcellars.com • info@comfortcellarswinery.com

Tastings, tours: Mon., Thu. and Fri. 10 a.m.-5 p.m.; Sat. 10 a.m.-6 p.m.; Sun. noon-5 p;m; tours by appointment.
Varieties: Cabernet Sauvignon, Chenin Blanc, Pinot Noir; sweet blends; dessert and novelty wines.

Across from the post office in downtown Comfort, a quaint, antiques-shop-clogged Hill Country town northwest of San Antonio, Comfort Cellars is a block from the historic district. The tasting room, in a century-old Hill Country home, also offers handmade soaps and other gifts for sale.

Comfort Cellars makes unusual novelty wines such as orange Chardonnay and raisin dessert wines, a peach wine and a jalapeño wine. It's on the Texas Hill Country Wineries and Guadalupe Valley wine trails.

Worth stopping for/overnighting: See **Bending Branch Winery** listing, page 16.

Driftwood Estate Winery

6 miles south of Dripping Springs, 1/4 mile east of RR 12 on CR 170 (Elder Hill Road).

4001 Elder Hill Road (County Road 170), Driftwood
512-858-9667 • www.driftwoodvineyards.com
info@driftwoodvineyards.com

Tastings, tours: Daily 10 a.m.-6 p.m. (except major holidays); tasting fee.
Varieties: Cabernet Sauvignon, Chardonnay, Merlot rosé and sweet blush wines, Syrah, Sangiovese and red blends.

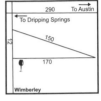

Just west of Austin between Wimberley and Dripping Springs, this winery is built on a hilltop that affords beautiful Hill Country vistas — with picnic tables, a pavilion and a large covered deck from which to enjoy them. Visitors are invited to bring a picnic for alfresco dining on the deck.

The 20-acre vineyard was planted in 1998 by Kathy and Gary Elliott, with the winery opening in 2003. Production has risen from 1,200 cases to more than 4,500 since then. Driftwood has won lots of fans for its Cabernets, Sangioveses and Orange Muscats.

The winery offers free wi-fi, occasional live music and special-occasion dinners, as well as themed events in the Texas Hill Country Wineries series. Private tastings, weddings and special events can be held under a large tent, and an event center accommodates 50.

Worth stopping for: See **Bell Springs Winery** listing, page 15.

Dry Comal Creek Vineyards and Winery

6.6 miles west of New Braunfels just off Texas 46 on Herbelin Road

1741 Herbelin Road, New Braunfels • 830-885-4076
www.drycomalcreek.com • inquire@drycomalcreek.com

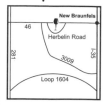

Tastings, tours: Daily noon-5 p.m. (except major holidays); tours 1:30 and 3 p.m. Sat.-Sun. Tasting and tour fees. Wheelchair-accessible.

Varieties: Cabernet Sauvignon, French Colombard (dry and demisweet), Lenoir (Black Spanish), Merlot, Orange Muscat, Petit Verdot, Syrah, red blends and a Black Spanish blush, plus sweet and dry sparkling wines and port- and sherry-style fortified wines.

In a small, protected valley in the Texas Hill Country, this little winery has battled Mother Nature in the form of floods and two devastating infestations of Pierce's disease, which destroyed its vines. It now makes its wine from grapes and juice from Texas, New Mexico, Arizona, Washington and Oregon but strives to put a Texas stamp on the flavor, mouthfeel and finish.

"We do not make a California-style wine," tasting room manager Sabrina Houser asserts. "We do not make a French-style wine. This does not mean our wines are not good. It means that they are different."

Dry Comal hosts "Winery U!" classes, dinners and other events and participates in Texas Hill Country Wineries events. Its event center is available for celebrations, gatherings and corporate functions.

Worth stopping for: New Braunfels' Conservation Plaza (830-629-2943, www.nbconservation.org) has numerous historic structures that give the community its special flavor. The **Gruene Historic District,** with its boutiques and access to the Guadalupe River, is a must-see. River outfitters rent tubes and rafts, and there's good barbecue and other fare nearby (www.gruenetexas.com). The fabled **Gruene Hall,** Texas' oldest dance hall, brings in name acts (830-606-1281, www.gruenehall.com).

Overnighting: In New Braunfels, **Prince Solms Inn** (830-625-9169, www.princesolmsinn.com) and **Hotel Faust** (830-625-7791, www.fausthotel.com) are two centrally located restored historic hostelries, the latter housing a brewpub. The New Braunfels Conservation Society operates the **Gerlich-Wagenfuehr B&B** (830-629-2943, www.nbconservation.org) downtown. In Gruene, **Gruene Mansion Inn** is a B&B housed in a gracefully imposing Victorian on the river (830-629-2641, www.gruenemansioninn.com).

Duchman Family Winery

Southwest of Austin on FM 150 a couple of miles south of Driftwood. From Austin, take U.S. 290 west toward Fredericksburg. At the third light, turn left on FM 1826 and go 14 miles until FM 1826 ends at FM 150. Turn left and go 2.3 miles.

13308 Farm-to-Market Road 150 W., Driftwood • 512-858-1470
http://duchmanwinery.com • michele@duchmanwines.com

Tastings, tours: Tastings Mon. noon-6 p.m., Tue.-Sat. 11 a.m.-9 p.m., Sun. noon-8 p.m. Tours Sat.-Sun. on the hour noon-7 p.m., or by reservation. Tasting/tour fees.

Dining: Trattoria Lisina open Sun. and Tue.-Thu. 11 a.m.-9 p.m., Fri.-Sat. 11 a.m.-10 p.m.; reservations 512-894-3111.

Varieties: Aglianico, Dolcetto, Montepulciano, Moscato, Orange Muscat, Pinot Grigio, Sangiovese, Syrah, Trebbiano, Vermentino, Zinfandel and blends; also planted are Barbera and Nero d'Avola grapes.

When it opened in 2004 under the Mandola name, this ambitious operation, with its stately Italianate villa and grounds, was under the aegis of Houston restaurateur Damian Mandola (Carrabba's) and two friends, Stan and Lisa Duchman, who had joined together to produce traditional Italian wines.

Now the winery, one of the most respected in Texas, is run by the Duchmans, while Mandola and his wife operate the Italian restaurant, Trattoria Lisina, next door. The Duchmans' wine distribution company, D'Amore Wine Selections, is also based at the winery.

The vineyard contains 20 acres of Montepulciano, Moscato, Barbera, Sangiovese, Vermentino, Nero d'Avola and Aglianico grapes on a slope above Onion Creek in a climate not unlike that of southern Italy. The Duchmans, however, source the majority of their grapes from carefully vetted growers in Texas' High Plains.

The Duchmans' wines — most of which, by the way, are quite reasonably priced — have attracted much buzz in the last few years, especially the Vermentino, a traditional Italian white wine. *Wine Enthusiast* magazine, among others, has singled out Duchman for praise.

The winery's tasting room sells all the Duchman wines, wine accessories, cookbooks, Italian olive oils, olives, pastas and more. It also carries a small selection of meat and cheese for picnicking and serves appetizers to pair with the wine. The winery, which is on the Texas Hill Country Wineries trail, frequently hosts musical evenings and art shows, and the event center and grounds are available for special events.

Worth stopping for: See listings for **Bella Vista Cellars**, page 14; **Bell Springs Winery**, page 15; and **Driftwood Estate Winery,** page 19.

Fall Creek Vineyards

2.2 miles north of Tow's post office, near Lake Buchanan.

1820 County Road 222, Tow • **Winery:** 325-379-5361
Corporate office: 512-476-4477 • www.fcv.com • info@fcv.com

Tastings, tours: Mon. Fri. 11 a.m.-4 p.m., Sat. 11 a.m.-5 p.m., Sun. noon-4 p.m.
Varieties: Cabernet Sauvignon, Chardonnay, Chenin Blanc, Merlot, Muscat Canelli, Riesling, Sauvignon Blanc, Viognier and blends, including the big meritage-style Meritus.

Set in the scenic Texas Hill Country on the northeastern shore of Lake Buchanan, the winery and vineyards began in 1975 as a pioneer in the rebirth of the state's wine industry on the Auler family's Fall Creek Ranch. The Aulers believed the ranch's microclimate, with its cool breezes from Lake Buchanan, comparable to those of some of the finest French wine-growing areas.

Hundreds of awards later, Fall Creek has built a reputation for combining the latest growing and winemaking techniques to produce some of the state's most loved wines, including its celebrated and much-medaled Meritus. These days, the Aulers say, demand outstrips supply for the products of the vineyard's 65 trellised acres. Plaudits for the winery include mentions in *The Los Angeles Times* ("one of the state's best and most consistent"), *Wine Spectator*, *The Wine Advocate* and *Gourmet* magazine. Winemaker/patriarch Ed Auler has been called the Robert Mondavi of Texas.

The Aulers produce wine under several labels: Fall Creek; Meritus; the accessible Twin Springs; and Mission de San Antonio Valero, part of whose proceeds goes to restoration of the Alamo. They also own the Perfect 10 California line.

Picnickers are welcome at the handsome ranch-based winery and vineyards, and boat cruises are an appealing option, lake level permitting. The winery sells Fall Creek condiments made with its wines, as well as other gifts.

Check its website for events, including Texas Hill Country Wineries events.

Worth stopping for: Vanishing Texas River Cruise, boarding 4 miles west of Burnet, offers 2-1/2-hour wildlife-viewing trips on the Colorado River. For required reservations: 800-474-8374, 512-756-6986 or vtrcinfo@vtrc.com. Website: www.vtrc.com. **Longhorn Cavern State Park,** in Burnet County, is a longtime destination for locals (877-441-2283, www.longhorncaverns.com or http://www.stateparks.com/longhorn_cavern.html). Nine miles east of Llano on Texas 29, a family of **bald eagles** nests each year in a tree along the Llano River. The nesting season is generally from late October to mid-March, and the nest is visible from the highway. Especially after the young birds have been born, you can find the spot by looking for the parked cars and photographers. In Llano, **Cooper's Old Time Pit Barbecue** is a revered Texas institution (915-247-5713). Numerous outdoor recreation opportunities — swimming, fishing, boating, scuba-diving, water-skiing, hiking, bird-watching, hunting, golfing and more — are afforded around the **Highland Lakes area** (www.thehighlandlakes.org).

Overnighting: The Antlers (Kingsland) is a 1901 inn, a former railroad resort that now includes cabins, cabooses and a private coach, on Lake LBJ (800-383-0007, www.theantlers.com). **Airy Mount B&B** (Burnet) offers great Hill Country views and gourmet breakfasts (512-756-4149, www.airymount.com). Lodging options abound in the **Highland Lakes** area, from resorts to lake houses to cabins and condos (www.highlandlakes.org).

FawnCrest Vineyard

Between San Antonio and Austin on Canyon Lake. From Austin, south on I-35 to RM 12 West (Texas 80) toward Luling/Wimberley; right on RR 12 to RR 32, left on FM 3424, right on FM 306, left on Cranes Mill Road, slight left on Canyon Shores, right on Westside Circle.

1370 Westside Circle, Canyon Lake
830-935-2407 • www.fawncrest.com • fawncrest@hotmail.com

Tastings, tours: Sat. noon-7 p.m.; other days by appointment.
Varieties: Cabernet Franc, Cabernet Sauvignon, Chardonnay, Merlot and meritage-style blends, from estate-grown and imported grapes.

Overlooking Comal County's Canyon Lake in the foothills of the Texas Hill Country, FawnCrest is 48 miles from San Antonio and 56 miles from Austin. Tastings are offered on the breezeway with its lake view.

Wine is sold on premises; FawnCrest's vision is to remain a small, family-run business producing high-quality dry wines at reasonable prices.

Worth stopping for: Tubing, rafting, canoeing, kayaking and camping are popular on the **Guadalupe River** (www.guadaluperiver.com). There's boating and fishing at **Canyon Lake,** which has a year-round temperature of 68 degrees, a man-made white-sand beach and a scenic river drive.

Fiesta Vineyard and Winery

Between Lometa and Bend. From Lampasas, take FM 580 west about 18 miles; winery is on the left.

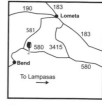

18727 W. Farm-to-Market Road 580, Lometa
325-628-3433 or 3434 • www.fiestawinery.com

Tours, tastings: Fri.-Sat. 10 a.m.-6 p.m., Sun. noon-5 p.m. Tasting fee (refunded with purchase).
Varieties: Cabernet Sauvignon, Merlot, Muscat Blanc, Pinot Gris, Pinot Noir, Riesling, Tempranillo, Zinfandel; blends both dry and sweet.

This fledgling Texas-flavored winery cozies up to the Colorado River on a 150-year-old homestead where the Baxter family and their forebears ranched and harvested pecans before planting varietal wine grapes.

"We want everyone to come out here and relax," says Sally Baxter. "You can sit at the tables inside or make yourself comfortable outside on the patio by the pool." The family encourages folks to bring a picnic basket and enjoy the countryside. Along with its wines, Fiesta offers trays of cheese, sausage, olives and crackers. The winery also hosts weddings, showers, reunions and other special events.

Worth stopping for/overnighting: See **Alamosa Wine Cellars** listing, page 10.

Flat Creek Estate

Off RM 1431 between Marble Falls and Lago Vista. From 1431, turn south on Singleton Bend Road and go 2 1/2 miles to Singleton Bend East; turn left, go 3/4 mile to the bottom of the hill; vineyard is on the left. Drive up the gravel road 1/8 mile to the gated entrance.

24912 Singleton Bend E., Marble Falls • 512-267-6310
www.flatcreekestate.com • wines@flatcreekestate.com

Tastings, tours: Tue.-Fri. noon-5 p.m., Sat. 10 a.m.-5 p.m., Sun. noon-5 p.m. Tasting fee. Group tastings and private dinners by appointment.
Dining: Bistro meals Fri.-Sun 11 a.m.-4 p.m.; cheese plates in Trooper's Den wine bar Fri.-Sun. noon-5 p.m.
Varieties: Muscat Canelli, Orange Muscat, Pinot Blanc, Pinot Grigio, Sangiovese, Tempranillo, Viognier and blends; port-style fortified wine, dessert wines, sparkling almond, sparkling raspberry

The owners must be nice folks. Sixty friends and relatives turned out in April 2000 to plant 6,000 vines on six acres in six hours flat — and volunteers have helped out with planting and harvesting ever since. Meanwhile, Flat Creek has expanded steadily in both size and reputation.

Rick and Madelyn Naber, Iowa transplants, have done their best to recreate a corner of Italy's famed Tuscany in the Texas Hill Country. And why not? Italian varietals seem to thrive in their pastoral vineyards. Flat Creek is known for its "Super Texan" Sangiovese, as well as for its Moscato d'Arancia, Moscato Blanco and Mistello dessert wine, now made by winemaker Tim Drake.

Nestled on a 20-acre scenic hillside not far from Travis Peak in the Texas Hill Country, the winery opened in April 2002 and began selling wines produced with grapes from other Texas growers under the Travis Peak Select label. From 2003, Flat Creek's own grapes have been used in its Flat Creek Estate Reserve wines, and one from that year, the Tuscan-style Sangiovese blend the Nabers dubbed their "Super Texan," won a double gold medal with a unanimous jury vote at the San Francisco International Wine Competition. More recently, the 2010 Viognier won a double gold at the 2011 San Francisco competition.

There's more than just wine. Reserve a place for a Tuscan-style weekend lunch or dinner, then a self-guided tour through the estate's vineyard trail. Or enjoy occasional live music, or a First Saturday wine dinner. Flat Creek also offers a handsome setting for weddings and other events, and it's on the Texas Hill Country Wineries trail.

In October 2006, *Food & Wine* magazine listed Flat Creek among "America's 50 Most Amazing Wine Experiences," lauding Flat Creek's output as "arguably Texas's best wines."

Worth stopping for: The resort community of **Horseshoe Bay**, on **Lake LBJ**, is an upscale playground offering resorts, golf courses, marinas, boating, fishing and other recreation. The other **Highland Lakes** are nearby, affording numerous recreation options — fishing, boating, water-skiing, swimming, picnicking, hiking, golfing, hunting, bird-watching and more. The influx of the moneyed into the area has changed Marble Falls, too, bringing in boutiques and such, but the **Bluebonnet Café** remains as it has always been: a venerable and frequently packed eatery famous for its made-in-house pies, with breakfast served all day (830-693-2344). **Sweet Berry Farm** (Marble Falls) offers "pick-your-own" berries and flowers; vegetables for sale; a hayfield maze, animals for petting and other family activities (830-798-1462). **Longhorn Cavern State Park,** south of Burnet, offers guided tours of the cavern; hiking trails; and history, nature and geology study programs (877-441-2283, www.tpwd.state.tx.us/spdest/findadest/parks/longhorn_cavern/). **Vanishing Texas River Cruise**, boarding 4 miles west of Burnet, offers 2-1/2-hour wildlife-viewing trips on the Colorado River. For required reservations: 800-474-8374, 512-756-6986 or vtrcinfo@vtrc.com.website: www.vtrc.com. **The Austin Steam Train** runs excursions on a scenic route from Cedar Park to Bertram and Burnet and back on Saturdays and for special themed excursions; the Burnet trips include a costumed gunfight.

Overnighting: The Antlers (Kingsland) is a 1901 inn, a former railroad resort that now includes cabins, cabooses and a private coach, on Lake LBJ (800-383-0007, www.theantlers.com). **Airy Mount B&B** (Burnet) offers great Hill Country views and gourmet breakfasts (512-756-4149, www.airymount.com). The **Highland Lakes** area abounds with resorts, lodges, cabins, cottages, lake houses and other accommodations (www.highlandlakes.org).

4.0 Cellars

On U.S. 290 east of Fredericksburg.

10354 E. U.S. 290, Fredericksburg
830-997-7470 • www.fourpointwine.com

Tastings: Mon.-Sat. 10 a.m.-6 p.m., Sun. noon-5 p.m. Tasting fee; complimentary wine glass with flight of six wines.

This new tasting room brings the wines of three respected winemakers — Kim McPherson of Lubbock's McPherson Cellars, Pat Brennan of Comanche's Brennan Vineyards and Gene Estes of Burleson's Lone Oak Vineyards — together in one tasting room.

The partners are stocking their own labels at 4.0 and are on the road to producing wines under the 4.0 label at the new tasting room — sherry and/or port, most likely.

The trio has built a refreshingly clean and modern building quite different from the typical faux-Tuscan Texas winery look, with a tower entrance, a large covered porch and shaded pavilion, an outdoor wine bar and a 5,000-square-foot tasting room and event facility. Also on the grounds is a small demonstration vineyard as well as space for picnicking under the live oaks. Snack are available.

For more information on the wines and the partner wineries, see listings for McPherson on page 63 of the "Panhandle Plains and West Texas" section and for Brennan on page 72 and Lone Oak on page 83 of the "North Central Texas" section.

Worth stopping for/overnighting: See **Becker Vineyards** listing, page 11.

Fredericksburg Winery

In Fredericksburg's historic downtown area.

247 W. Main St., Fredericksburg • 830-990-8747
www.fbgwinery.com • wine@fbgwinery.com

Tastings, tours: Mon.-Thu. 10 a.m.-5 p.m.; Fri.-Sat. 10 a.m.-7:30 p.m.; Sun. noon-5:30 p.m. (hours may vary). Fees charged for groups of 10 or more.
Varieties: Gewürztraminer, Merlot, Muscat Canelli, Muscat Hamburg, Orange Muscat, Sangiovese, port-style fortified wine, blends.

The German-flavored Hill Country community of Fredericksburg, named for Prince Frederick of Prussia, has a wealth of boutiques and wineries, including this 10,600-square-foot operation right smack-dab in town on Main Street. Interested in a late-harvest dessert wine? This is the place.

The Switzer family concentrates on specialty wines, making them in small case lots and buying only Texas-grown grapes — mostly from the High Plains — and this little-winery-that-could has earned some national media attention. On the Texas Hill Country Wineries and Fredericksburg Wine Road 290 trails, it participates in those groups' seasonal events.

Worth stopping for/overnighting: See **Becker Vineyards** listing, page 11.

Georgetown Winery and Vineyard

Downtown Georgetown, east side of the courthouse.

715 S. Main St., Georgetown • 512-869-8600
www.georgetownwinery.com • texaswinery@yahoo.com

Tastings, tours: Tue.-Thu. 11 a.m. - 6 p.m., Fri.-Sat.11 a.m.-8 p.m., Sun. 12:30-5:30 p.m. Fee.
Varieties: Barolo, Cabernet Sauvignon, Chardonnay, Malbec, Merlot, Petit Verdot, Pinot Grigio, Pinot Noir, Sangiovese, Sauvignon Blanc, Sémillon, Shiraz, Zinfandel; apple, blackberry, blueberry and peach sweet wines; port-style fortified wines; ice wine; honey mead; blends.

Situated on Georgetown's increasingly cute courthouse square, this is a storefront make-your-own wine operation that can be taken seriously. Within two years of opening, Dan and Becca Marek began taking home medals for their wine, especially their dessert wines, at competitions.

The couple moved from Rockdale, seeing in downtown Georgetown the right sort of location for their venture. Needless to say, the winery's award-winning Chocolate Cherry Port was something new to Williamson County, and perhaps to the rest of Texas. The Mareks source the majority of their grapes from Texas, with the rest from California.

The Mareks invite you to sit a spell, enjoy a cheese tray and sample from their abundant list of on-premise-made wines. And maybe Dan will tell you how he learned how to make wine as a child.

Live music from 5 to 8 p.m. every Friday and Saturday.

Worth stopping for: Georgetown's downtown is considered one of the prettiest in Texas (http://visit.georgetown.org/); the **Palace Theatre** offers live productions (512-869-7469, www.georgetownpalace.com). Georgetown's **Williamson Museum** runs a Chisholm Trail cattle drive and chuckwagon cook off each September and other pioneer-themed events (716 S. Austin Ave., 512-943-1670). Fine-dining options include **La Maison French Cuisine & Patisserie** (512-868-8885, www.lamaisontx.com) and **Wildfire** (512-869-3473, www.wildfiretexas.com). **Berry Springs Park and Preserve** offers camping, fishing and a 2.5-mile hike/bike trail (512-260-4283). The **Austin Steam Train** runs excursions on a scenic route from nearby Cedar Park to Bertram and Burnet and back on Saturdays and for special themed excursions; the Burnet trips include a costumed gunfight by the **Burnet Gunfighters** (512-477-8468, www.austinsteamtrain.org).

Grape Creek Vineyards

U.S. 290 at South Grape Creek, 4 miles west of Stonewall, 9 miles east of Fredericksburg.

10587 E. U.S. 290, Fredericksburg • 830-644-2710
www.grapecreek.com • relax@grapecreek.com

Winery tastings, tours: Mon.-Fri.11 a.m.-6 p.m., Sat. 10 a.m.-6 p.m., Sun.11 a.m.-5 p.m. Fee.
Grape Creek on Main: Downtown Fredericksburg tasting room, Fredericksburg Art Gallery, 314 E. Main St.: Mon.-Sat. 10 a.m.-5:30 p.m., Sun. noon-5 p.m.
Varieties: Merlot, Muscat Canelli, Pinot Grigio, Viognier; port-style fortified wine; red, white and sweet blends.

Four miles west of Stonewall, in a spot selected for its beneficial micro-climate, the winery's 17 acres of vinifera vines are planted on rolling hills that are also home to the area's famous peach trees, an herb garden and a blackberry patch.

Grape production began in 1985, and after a nearby winery did well with its harvest, Grape Creek decided to produce its own wines, building the winery in 1989. A year later, the owners created the first Texas underground wine cellar, an on-grounds villa for overnight stays and a gift shop.

The Villa on Grape Creek, renovated in 2008, has two bedrooms, each with queen bed and private bathroom. The 1,200-square-foot building includes a full kitchen, breakfast nook, writing desk, sitting room and views of the vineyards; a wine tasting and bottle of wine are complimentary.

After Brian Heath bought the winery in 2006, four new vineyard blocks were planted in Montepulciano, Aglianico, Chenin Blanc and Petit Verdot grapes. The residence was transformed into a Tuscan-style tasting room and event center with a tree-shaded patio, rock bell tower and wall. A recent expansion added a wine library with all Grape Creek vintages, converted the old tank room into a barrel room and added a new tank room.

"The massive stucco structure with the tile roof is nestled in a copse of gnarled live oak trees that gives the setting the feel of 'Tuscany in Texas,' " the *San Antonio Express-News* said in 2008.

Winemaker Jason Englert works with grapes from Grape Creek's own vineyards as well as other Texas vineyards and grapes from New Mexico's Mesilla Valley. The winery enters numerous wine competition and brings home medals from most.

Grape Creek's wines can also be found in its downtown Fredericksburg tasting room, Grape Creek on Main, which shares spaces with the Fredericksburg Art Gallery.

The winery participates in many of the Texas Hill Country Wineries (www.texaswinetrail.com) and Fredericksburg Wine Road 290 (www.wineroad290.com) events.

Indeed, with three tasting rooms — 4.0 Cellars, Mendelbaum Cellars and Messina Hof Hill Country — having opened close by, Grape Creek's little piece of U.S. 290 is becoming a veritable wine oasis.

Worth stopping for: The Hill Country towns of **Stonewall, Luckenbach, Johnson City** and **Blanco** are nearby. **Lyndon B. Johnson National Historical Park** comprises two parks, one in Johnson City, with a visitor center, Johnson's boyhood home and the Johnson Settlement, and the LBJ Ranch 14 miles west of Johnson City near Stonewall (830-868-7128, www.nps.gov/lyjo). Several **lavender farms** can be found near Johnson City; check www.johnson citytexaschamber. com/things_to_do/index.html. **Pedernales Falls State Park**, in Blanco County east of Johnson City, offers camping, picnicking, hiking, river swimming, tubing, wading, mountain biking, fishing, bird-watching (830-868-7304, http://www.tpwd.state.tx.us/spdest/findadest/parks/pederna-les_falls/). For Fredericksburg attractions, see **Becker Vineyards**, page 11.

Overnighting: Rose Hill Manor (Stonewall), a replica of an Old South plantation house, is an inn with four suites, a reputation for fine dining and a beautiful view of the Pedernales River Valley (830-644-2247, www.rose-hill.com). The stately **Chantilly Lace Country Inn Bed & Breakfast** in Johnson City offers six acres of gardens, including a lavender field, verandas, porches, a pavilion and a restaurant open to the public (830-660-2621 or 830-637-9080, www.chantillylacesoaps.com). For Fredericksburg lodging, see **Becker Vineyards**, page 11.

Hilmy Cellars

About 11 miles east of downtown Fredericksburg, near Stonewall, on U.S. 290: Driving east, the winery is on the left about a half-mile past the sign for Becker Vineyards.

12346 E. U.S. 290, Fredericksburg • 830-644-2482
www.hilmywine.com

Tours, tastings: Daily 11 a.m.-6 p.m. Fee (waived with purchase).
Varieties: Muscat Canelli, Tempranillo and blends (check website for updates).

Another in the burgeoning enclave of wineries on U.S. 290 east of Fredericksburg, this new winery is home to a flock of guinea fowl for insect control, two Great Pyrenees dogs for deer control and a goat herd for weed control.

Owner Erik Hilmy made wine on an amateur basis for a dozen years before deciding to go pro, joking that "it's the only thing I've been consistently good at in my life." His goal at Hilmy, he says, "is to try to make the best wine we know how."

To that end, he says, he'll be sourcing his grapes not just from Texas but from wherever "we find the quality to be there," be it California, Washington, Italy or South America.

From Texas, he's using High Plains grapes from Andy Timmons' vineyard in Terry County and has planted a 3-acre vineyard of Sangiovese and Tempranillo at the winery. Next will come another 3 acres of white grapes such as Vermentino, Picpoul Blanc and Rousanne, he says, with the eventual goal of making and selling estate wines. But "we're not shy about the fact that we make wine that's not from Texas," because for him, how the wine tastes is more important than where the grapes came from.

He wanted a "rustic/urban" feel for his tasting room, which has concrete floors and exposed beams, a courtyard for seating, an olive grove, bocce ball courts and a pizza oven. Locally made charcuterie and cheeses are available.

Check the website for events and updates.

Worth stopping for/overnighting: See listings for **Becker Vineyards**, page 11, and **Grape Creek Vineyards**, page 28.

Kerrville Hills Winery

Northeast of Kerrville on Texas 16 (Fredericksburg Road). From Interstate 10, take Exit 508, go north on Texas 16; drive 2.3 miles to the winery entrance on the left.

3600 Fredericksburg Road, Kerrville • 830-895-4233
www.kerrvillehillswinery.com • info@kerrvillehillswinery.com

Tastings, tours: Thu.-Sun 1-6 p.m., or by appointment.
Varieties: Blanc du Bois, Cabernet Sauvignon, Merlot.

Kerrville's first winery, opened in 2011, is situated on a 30-acre ranch overlooking the Guadalupe River Valley.

Owner and winemaker Wayne Milberger buys grapes from Brenham for his Blanc du Bois and from Lake County, Calif., for his Cabernet Sauvignon and Merlot. The winery had grabbed medals for its Cabernet Sauvignon and Merlot even before patrons had crossed its threshold.

Kerrville Hills has an expansive tasting room with a massive double-sided fireplace.

Worth stopping for: The **Guadalupe River** runs through Kerrville, and the city takes advantage of this with **Louise Hays Park**, on the river's banks downtown, with picnic tables and an island reached by a footbridge. The larger CCC-era **Kerrville-Schreiner Park**, with the river as its centerpiece, offers campsites and cabins and a full gamut of recreation (830-257-5392). Downtown art options include the **Kerr Arts & Cultural Center** (830-895-2911, www.kacckerrville.com) and the **Museum of Western Art** (830-896-2553, www.museumofwesternart.com). In west Kerr County, near Ingram, the **Hill Country Arts Foundation** offers theater performances, an art gallery and studios and the recently relocated **Stonehenge II**, a 60-percent-size replica of Stonehenge with some Easter Island heads thrown in (830-367-5120, www.hcaf.com). And the tiny town of **Hunt**, in western Kerr County, is home to the **Hunt Store**, with picnic-table seating, a nostalgic old-time grocery-store setting, frequent live music, Thursday night steak dinners and such surprising specialties as lobster rolls or peach brandy sorbet (1634 Texas 39, 830-238-4410).
Overnighting: South of Kerrville is an impressive new Italian-style villa that houses **"Texas Country Reporter" Bob Phillips' Escondida**, with its 10 guest rooms; spa, pool and workout

area; and a chef on staff offering breakfasts and dinners (888-589-7507, www.escondidaresort.com).

La Cruz de Comal Wines

From Austin, south on I-35, right on Texas 46, right on FM 2722

7405 Farm-to-Market Road 2722, Startzville • 830-899-2723
www.lacruzdecomalwines.com
lewis@lacruzdecomalwines.com

Tastings, tours: Noon-6 p.m. Sat.-Sun. and by appointment. Fee.
Varieties: Blanc du Bois, Malbec, Syrah; blends made from Alicante Bouchet, Cabernet Sauvignon, Lenoir (Black Spanish), Malbec, Merlot, Norton, Syrah, Tannat and Viognier.

This winery is the dream of a Houston lawyer named Lewis Dickson — with the help of California winemaker Tony Coturri — who initially kept it very low-profile. Word about their viticultural acumen got out when he entered a competition — and won a gold medal before the winery had even opened for business.

Dickson's small tasting room, with a roof of century-old clay tiles, is built from stone and cedar collected from his LD3 Ranch.

"We offer the real Texas-terroir thing: Texas grapes, fermentations on natural yeasts, no additions of acid, sugar, grape concentrate, powdered tannins, artificial coloring agents, reverse osmosis or any other form of hocus pocus," Dickson says. The results, bottled under the Cruz de Comal and Dickson labels, are highly regarded by wine buyers.

Lost Creek Vineyard

Between Austin and Llano. From Austin, take Loop 1 South, head west on Texas 71, take the Kingsland/Sunrise Beach exit, turn right on RR 2233.

1129 Ranch Road 2233, Sunrise Beach • 325-388-3753
www.lostcreekvineyard.com • lcvine@moment.net

Tastings, tours: Tue.-Sat. 4-9 p.m. (may change seasonally).
Dining: Tree House Bistro spring/summer hours Tue. Sun. 5-10 p.m., Sun. brunch 11 a.m.-3 p.m.; fall-winter hours Wed.-Sat. 4-9 p.m. (happy hour 4-5:30 p.m.).
Varieties: Blanc du Bois, Chardonnay, red and white blends.

This enchantingly situated winery is tucked into a scenic corner of the Hill Country. Geese gather on the grounds, an oasis for butterflies and migratory birds on the Central Flyover route.

The winery was almost destroyed by major flooding in 2007, but owners David and Valerie Brinkman rebuilt and reopened in 2008. An ornate, lovingly restored 55-foot-long 19th-century bar graces Lost Creek's new 7,600-square-foot tasting room and restaurant, the Tree House Bistro, which offers a Southwestern-leaning menu, a full bar and live music on weekends in peak visiting season.

The winery also includes a visitors' area, an amphitheater for its concert series and a peaceful pond, home to six species of frogs. Indeed, the winery has taken for its mascot a Texas tree frog, dubbed Hopper. After sampling the wines, you can visit the swans in the creek; if you can't tear yourself away, Lost Creek has added a bed and breakfast with handsomely furnished lodgings.

Worth stopping for/overnighting: See **Fall Creek Vineyards** listing, page 22, and **Flat Creek Estate** listing, page 24.

McReynolds Wines

40 miles west of Austin; 6 miles east of U.S. 281 between highways 71 and 290. From U.S. 281, go east on FM 962 (Round Mountain Road) to Shovel Mountain Road.

706 Shovel Mountain Road, Cypress Mill • 830-825-3544
www.mcreynoldswines.com • mcreynoldswines@hillcountrytx.net

Tastings, tours: Fri.-Sat. 10 a.m.-6 p.m., Sun. noon-6 p.m. and by appointment.
Varieties: Cabernet Sauvignon, Chardonnay, Merlot.

Come by for a visit and an informal tasting with winemakers Maureen and Mac McReynolds, who learned the craft in California while keeping their day jobs, in scientific research at Stanford University.

They began as home winemakers, but after winning two gold medals for their '05 Texas Shiraz, the McReynoldses decided to make the leap and turn their Hill Country retreat into a commercial winery. They purchase grapes from around Texas and are growing their own on four of their acres.

When the weather is good, you can bring a picnic lunch and enjoy the wine under the winery's oaks. Visitors to the winery, 40 miles west of Austin on the Texas Hill Country Wineries trail, may be greeted by two dogs, Blanca and Sangria, and a cat named Earl Grey.

Worth stopping for: See **Bell Springs**, page 15.

Mendelbaum Cellars

On U.S. 290 just east of Fredericksburg.

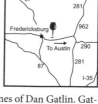

10207 E. U.S. 290, Fredericksburg
830-997-7000 • www.mendelbaumcellars.com

Tastings: Fri.-Sat. 10 a.m.-8 p.m., Sun. 11 a.m.-6 p.m., Mon. and Wed.-Thu. 10 a.m.-6 -p.m.; closed Tue. Tasting fee.

A two-story cottage has been transformed from a restaurant into a new tasting room showcasing the wines of Dan Gatlin. Gatlin's two labels — Inwood Estates, based in Dallas, and Vineyard at Florence — rank among some of Texas' most sought-after wines, and he'll be producing a lower-priced Mendelbaum Cellars label for the tasting room.

Mendelbaum isn't Gatlin's project; he explains that he has granted owner Nitzan Mendelbaum exclusive rights to sell his wine — highly ranked by those in the know — in Gillespie County.

The tasting room also will offer gourmet picnic goodies such as cheeses, charcuterie and mustards, along with a selection of Texas beers.

For more information on Gatlin's wines, see listings for Inwood, on page 80 of the "North Central Texas" section, and the Vineyard at Florence, on page 53 of the "Hill Country and Central Texas" section.

Worth stopping for/overnighting: See **Becker Vineyards** listing, page 11.

Pedernales Cellars

South of U.S. 290 between Fredericksburg and Johnson City. From 290, go south on South Ranch Road 1623 for 1 1/2 miles. Turn right on Upper Albert Road just before 1623 curves sharply left.

2916 Upper Albert Road, Stonewall
830-644-2050, 830-644-2037
www.pedernalescellars.com • info@pedernalescellars.com

Tastings, tours: Mon.-Thu. 10 a.m.-5 p.m., Fri.-Sat. 10 a.m.-6 p.m., Sun. noon-6 p.m. Tasting fee (waived with wine purchase).

Cellar tours on the half-hour Fri.-Sun., starting at 12:30 p.m.; private tours by appointment.
Varieties: Cabernet Sauvignon, Garnacha rosé, Merlot, Muscat Canelli, Tempranillo, Viognier, blends.

This winery, 17 miles from Fredericksburg on the Fredericksburg Wine Road 290 wine trail, was opened more than a decade and a half after the first vines were planted in the family's Kuhlken Vineyards in the early 1990s. The estate vineyard, expanded over the years, now encompasses 17 acres of mainly warm-weather varieties like Tempranillo, Touriga Nacional, Monastrell (Mourvèdre) and Garnacha (Grenache), as well as Cabernet Sauvignon and Merlot.

A two-generation family operation — three, during harvests and crush — Pedernales Cellars broke ground on the 15,000-square-foot winemaking facility in 2007, finishing the 4,000-square-foot underground barrel room in time for the 2008 crush. In less than a year, Pedernales had won its first medal.

Visitors are encouraged to roam the grounds, enjoy the calm and take in the views of the valley and Gingerbread Hill with a glass of wine from the tree-shaded deck.

Worth stopping for/overnighting: See **Becker Vineyards** listing, page 11.

Perissos Vineyard and Winery

South of Inks Lake State Park off Texas 29 between Burnet and Llano. From Burnet, go west on Texas 29 (West Polk Street) for 2 miles; turn left at Hoover's Valley Road; go 8 miles to State Park Road 4 and turn left; the winery is about a half-mile south.

7214 Park Road 4 W., Burnet • 512-656-8419
www.perissosvineyards.com • Laura@PerissosVineyards.com

Tastings, tours: Fri.-Sun. noon-5 p.m.
Varieties: Petite Sirah, Malbec, Roussane, Viognier and blends including Aglianico, Chenin Blanc, Garnacha, Malbec, Mourvèdre, Muscat, Nero d'Avola, Syrah, Tempranillo, Touriga and Viognier.

Just south of Inks Lake State Park and nestled in the picturesque Hoover's Valley, this respected Texas Hill Country winery uses only Texas-grown grapes – 85 percent of them from its own 5000-plus vines.

The family-owned and -operated winery opened for business in spring of 2009, almost immediately winning recognition by medaling with its Roussanne blend, a white made of four grape varieties grown in its 13-acre vineyard.

Laura and Seth Martin used to build custom homes in Austin, where they began experimenting with growing their own grapes in their yard and making their own wine in their garage. As their interest grew, they gave up Austin for the country life. But the couple and their children went a bit further than most vintners, deciding halfway through preparations to live above the winery in a dramatic purpose-built stone building.

There's no dedicated tasting room yet, but visitors don't mind, says Laura. "We hold the tastings in the barrel room and the production room, and people like to be where the action is." It's on the Top of the Hill Country Wine Trail.

Bring a picnic lunch to enjoy with your wine under the many shade trees, then soak in the scenery of the 42-acre property and beyond. "Perissos" is Greek for "exceedingly abundant, beyond what is expected, imagined, or hoped for."

Worth stopping for: Inks Lake State Park offers camping, backpacking, hiking, a nine-hole golf course, swimming, boating, water skiing, scuba diving and fishing. The park hosts nature walks, geology hikes, fish seining and the Devil's Waterhole Canoe Tour (512-793-2223, www.tpwd. state.tx.us/spdest/findadest/parks/inks/). The other **Highland Lakes** are nearby. Also see **Fall Creek Vineyards** listing, page 22, and **Flat Creek Estate** listing, page 24.

Pillar Bluff Vineyards

3 1/2 miles southwest of Lampasas: From U.S. 281, take FM 1478 (Naruna Road) west of Lampasas for 3 miles to the Burnet County line, turning left onto CR 111 for 1/4 mile.

300 County Road 111, Lampasas • 512-556-4078
www.pillarbluff.com • vineyard@earth-comm.com

Tastings, tours: Fri.-Sat 10 a.m.-5 p.m., Sun. 12:30-5 p.m. or by appointment.
Varieties: Cabernet Sauvignon, Chardonnay, Chenin Blanc, Merlot, ruby port-style fortified wine and blends.

Just west of Lampasas, a little more than an hour northwest of Austin on the edge of the Hill Country, Pillar Bluff is on the Texas Hill Country Wineries, Way Out Wineries and Top of the Hill Country trails.

Sample its estate-grown vintages in the tasting room or outside in the shade of majestic live oaks and the new pavilion.

"Pillar Bluff Vineyards produces appealing wines," says the *Abilene Reporter-News*.

Worth stopping for: Hancock Springs Free Flow Pool, built in 1911 and fed by one of the sulphur springs that made Lampasas a spa destination in its early years, is still open in summer (512-556-6831). Nearby, on the banks of Sulphur Creek, are ruins of 1880s-era bathhouses, the 109-acre **Hancock Park** and **Hancock Park Golf Course** (512-556-3202). In Lampasas, **Storm's Drive-In** is a classic 1950-vintage burger stand, the original in a Hill Country mini-chain (512-556-6269, www.stormsrestaurants.com).
Overnighting: Airy Mount B&B (Burnet) offers great Hill Country views and gourmet breakfasts (512-756-4149, www.airymount.com).

Pilot Knob Vineyard

From Austin: Take Texas 183 north toward Georgetown; go left on FM 243 one mile, then right on CR 213 and left on CR 212 to the top of the hill.

3125 County Road 212, Bertram • 512-489-2999
www.pilotknobvineyard.com • info@pilotknobvineyard.com

Hours: Thu.-Mon. noon-6 p.m.; Tue.-Wed. by appointment. Tasting fee (waived with purchase).
Varieties: Cabernet Sauvignon, Viognier, sweet rosé and blends.

Even before it opened in the spring of 2011, Pilot Creek had won a gold medal for its Viognier at the Lone Star International Wine Competition while taking a silver and a bronze at the San Francisco International Wine Competition. The latter, especially, is no mean feat.

Pilot Knob was created after Craig Pinkley got the wine bug during a banking conference in the Napa Valley. As he delved more and more into the world of wine, he felt the pull of winemaking, and eventually he left the financial industry to create a vineyard and winery.

The establishment is named for a nearby volcanic formation; built on the edge of a ridgeline about 50 miles north of Austin, Pilot Knob offers views of rolling hills. And its large covered wrap-around veranda and patio mean visitors can enjoy the panorama while savoring Texas wines along with baguettes and cheese from the winery, or vittles they've brought along. There are indoor and outdoor fireplaces for cooler weather, plus reception and meeting rooms inside for private events.

"What we are doing is creating a sense of place around Pilot Knob and a relaxing wine experience," Pinkley says. Check the website for Saturday music events, from country to jazz and bossa nova. Pilot Knob is on the Top of the Hill Country Wine Trail.

Worth stopping for: The **Austin Steam Train's Bertram Flyer** excursion stops at the restored Bertram Depot on its run from Cedar Park on Saturdays (512-477-8468, www.austinsteamtrain. org). Also see **Fall Creek Vineyards** listing, page 22, and **Flat Creek Estate** listing, page 24.

Poteet Country Winery

From San Antonio: Go south on Texas 16 36 miles; turn right on CR 476, left on CR 2146, right on Tank Hollow Road.

400 Tank Hollow Road, Poteet • 830-276-8085
www.poteetwine.com • bobbydenson@msn.com

Tastings, tours: Fri.-Sun. noon-6 p.m., or by appointment; free.
Varieties: Blackberry, mustang grape, strawberry.

A little more than a half-hour south of San Antonio and deep in Texas strawberry country, this establishment produces the "official" wine of the annual Poteet Strawberry Festival — made, of course, from strawberries. Poteet Country's other wines are made from native mustang grapes and from blackberries.

Founders Jim Collums and Bob Denson insist on using only locally grown fruit at their winery, housed in an old dairy.

Also on the grounds is the General Store, furnished as a pre-Prohibition mercantile establishment and selling crafts along with the fruit wines, jams and home winemaking equipment. Around the property are old windmills and water towers. Picnickers are encouraged, and the grounds can be hired for special occasions.

Every November, the winery hosts its own Country Wine Festival with live entertainment, Dutch-oven chuckwagon food, "chicken roping," arts and crafts. Check the website for other events.

Worth stopping for: The **Poteet Strawberry Festival**, held every April, is one of Texas' oldest events. It provides abundant family entertainment, including a parade, fireworks, concerts, dance troupes, gunslingers, clowns, puppets, regional bands, contests and rodeo performances (830-742-8144).

Rancho Ponte Vineyard

5 miles east of Fredericksburg off U.S. 290, behind the KOA on the road to Luckenbach.

315 Ranch Road 1376, Fredericksburg
830-990-8555
www.ranchoponte.com • info@ranchoponte.com

Tastings, tours: Sun.-Fri. 11 a.m.-5 p.m., Sat. 11 a.m. 6 p.m. Tasting fee.

Varieties: Merlot, Sangiovese, Sauvignon Blanc and blends including Arneis, Cabernet Franc, Cabernet Sauvignon, Chardonnay, Cortese, Lagrein, Petit Verdot, Malbec, Mourvèdre, Muscat Canelli, Roussane, Viognier, plus a rosé, a port and a while port.

Surrounded by Hill Country cattle and horse ranches, this family-owned winery opened in February 2009 and offers each guest a Rancho-Ponte-emblazoned wine glass to take home after the tasting.

Owner-winemaker Robert Ponte is a fourth-generation wine grower; his family has owned vineyards in Italy and South America. At Rancho Ponte, he likes to play with blends, using "the best grapes we can purchase," including some not-so-well-known Italian varieties.

"We produce the kind of wine we like to drink on a daily basis with family and friends — fruit-forward, interesting and unorthodox blends worth talking about at the table," says Ponte, who worked with grapes and wine in California and Venezuela before heading to Texas.

"We are a small, hands-on operation, but we are not new at this," he points out. "We have been in the wine business, working for and with others, for many years, but decided to take the plunge and start our own independent family winery."

Worth stopping for: Made famous by Willie Nelson and his fun-loving crowd, **Luckenbach** is not much more than the 1849 general store/saloon, but this colorful Lilliputian community is worth a visit. There's some variety of laid-back live music most nights; check website for concerts in the dance hall: www.luckenbachtexas.com. The town hosts an annual Texas Independence Day celebration. From Luckenbach, follow Grapetown Road southwest to Old San Antonio Road and south to the **Old Tunnel Wildlife Management Area**, where from mid-May to mid-October millions of Mexican free-tail bats emerge from a long-abandoned railway tunnel (866-978-2287). Also see **Becker Vineyards** listing, page 11, and **Grape Creek Vineyards** listing, page 28.

Rising Star Vineyards

Rising Star and Salado

www.risingstarvineyards.com • moubre@txwinemark.com

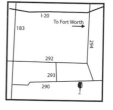

Rising Star tasting room

Five miles north of Rising Star. From Austin, go north on Texas 183 through Brownwood and Rising Star; turn right on CR 290; vineyard is 1 1/4 miles on the right. From the Metroplex or Abilene, take I-20 to Cisco, go south on Texas 183 for 15 miles, turn east on CR 290.

1001 County Road 290, Rising Star • 254-643-1776

Tastings, tours: Fri.-Sat. 11 a.m.-6 p.m., Sun. noon-4 p.m.

Salado tasting room

In downtown Salado just off Interstate 35 between Belton and Georgetown. From I-35 North, take exit No. 284 and turn left on Main Street; from I-35 South, take Salado exit to Main Street.

110 N. Main St., Salado • 254-947-5247

Tastings: Tue.-Fri. noon-6 p.m., Sat. noon-9 p.m., Sun. noon-4 p.m.
Varieties: Cabernet Sauvignon, Chardonnay, Merlot, Muscat, blends.

Rising Star Vineyards, which operates two vineyards in Central Texas, was established in 1999 with a small vineyard on the northern fringe of the Hill Country. After supplying other Texas operations, it began its own winemaking in 2005 and opened a small tasting room with gift shop at Rising Star in 2006 to sell its estate-grown wines.

In 2011, Rising Star opened an ambitious new tasting room in the historic stagecoach-stop town of Salado, where the grounds include a shaded garden and there's live music on Saturday nights. The winery also operates the Texas Cheesery next door, selling Texas products and serving cheese plates and other noshes.

Rising Star Vineyards participates in the Way Out Wineries weekend events and offers Sunday wine classes.

Worth stopping for: **Rising Star Trade Days,** fourth weekend of each month (254-643-1611). The **Turtle Restaurant, Enoteca and Gelateria** in Brownwood offers "slow fresh" chef-driven fare and showcases local ingredients and wines from the Way Out Wineries (325-646-8200, www.theturtlerestaurant.com).

Salado Creek Winery & Vineyard

Central Salado.

227 N. Main St., Salado • 254-947-9000
www.saladoswirlandsip.com
saladocreekwinery@centurylink.net

Tastings, tours: Open Mon.-Thu. noon-7 p.m., Fri. noon-8 p.m.,
Sat. noon-10 p.m., Sun. noon-5 p.m.; tastings till 5 each day.
Varieties: Cabernet Franc, Cabernet Sauvignon, Chardonnay,
Gewürtztraminer, Petit Verdot, Shiraz, Tempranillo, Vidal ice wine, port-style dessert wine, sweet
and dry blends; lemon, lime, honey mead and fruit-grape blends.

Salado Creek is another winery that has its origins in a passion for home
winemaking. It was born in 2009 from a little shop called Salado Swirl &
Sip, selling wine, winemaking and home-brewing supplies and gifts on Main
Street in the very visitor-friendly community of Salado. Now it calls itself the
town's first award-winning winery and cigar shop.

The move from wine shop to full-fledged winery was delayed in 2010
when Tropical Storm Hermine dropped 16 inches of rain, flooding Salado
Creek and washing away the winery's inventory and equipment and ruining
the building. The winery moved to its present location and opened its doors
in less than two months.

The winery has music on Saturday nights, bringing artists in from nearby
Austin, and on weekends food can be purchased to enjoy with the wines
crafted on site, which include fruit wines and a chocolate mandarin orange
port.

Worth stopping for: Salado (www.salado.com) makes much of its history as a stop on the
Chisholm Trail and is home to a number of art and craft galleries as well as gift shops, historic
sites and antiquey boutiques. Generations of travelers have stopped at the **Stagecoach Inn** for
a meal in the dining room or a stay in one of the rooms in the inn's complex adjacent to the **Mill
Creek Golf Course**. An unusual number of B&Bs, many overlooking the creek, include the **Inn at
Salado, the Inn on the Creek, Old Salado Springs** and the **Rose Mansion**.

Sandstone Cellars Winery

From Georgetown, go west on Texas 29 to downtown Mason; Sandstone Cellars is just southeast of the courthouse square on U.S. 87 (San Antonio Street).

211 San Antonio St., Mason • 325-347-9463
www.sandstonecellarswinery.com
wine@sandstonecellarswinery.com

Tastings, tours: Thu.-Sat. 11 p.m.-6 p.m., Sun. 11 p.m.-2 p.m.
Varieties: Touriga; red blends including Barbera, Grenache, Mourvèdre, Nebbiolo, Primitivo, Sangiovese, Syrah, Tempranillo, Viognier, Zinfandel; and a port-style dessert wine.

This winery, housed in a sandstone building, opened in October 2004 as part of a growing complex. The owners are a classically trained viola player, Scott Haupert, and a former Gap manager, Manny Silerio.

They run a casual but memorable eatery next door, Santos Taqueria, featuring Durango-style Mexican fare ("Not your meemaw's Tex-Mex") and an art gallery featuring paintings, jewelry and sculpture. They've recently added a wine bar with a pleasant porch in Lucia's Hacienda, the circa-1870 house of Lucia Holmes, whose diary of pioneer life in 19th-century Mason County is something of a local classic.

Mason County boasts a growing reputation among Texas viticulturists as a source of Mediterranean varietals, and Sandstone uses only grapes grown in the Hickory Sand Aquifer of Mason and McCulloch counties, situated on the very northernmost edge of the Hill Country. One of those grape growers, the highly respected Don Pullum of Akashic Vineyard, is their winemaker, and Sandstone Cellars sells other Texas wines as well. Sandstone specializes in red blends, and its wines, named by Roman numerals, are quite sought-after by Texas wine aficionados.

Texas Monthly called Santos Taqueria one of the 25 treasures of the Hill Country, but the winery bids fair to eclipse the restaurant's renown: In the latest edition of "Parker's Wine Buyer's Guide," wine superguru Robert Parker featured Sandstone among six Texas wineries as particularly worthy of note.

Worth stopping for: The Eckert James River Bat Cave Preserve southwest of Mason is one of the country's largest bat nurseries: About 4 million female bats and their offspring live there during the summer months. It's open to visitors mid-May through early October; call ahead at 325-347-5970. On Mason's downtown square, the old **Odeon Theater** is being restored, showing movies on weekends and hosting occasional concerts (325-347-9010, www.theodeontheater.com).

42

SantaMaria Cellars

Between Fredericksburg and Kerrville on Texas 16.

12044 Texas 16 S., Fredericksburg
830-998-5357, 830-515-9903
www.santamariacellarswines.com

Tastings, tours: Fri.-Sat. noon- 6 p.m.
Varieties: Cabernet Sauvignon, Malbec, Merlot, Pinot Noir, Muscat Canelli, Pinot Grigio, port and dessert wines and blends.

This may be a relatively new winery, but its Argentine-born namesake founder and winemaker Martin Santamaria comes with plenty of the right kind of baggage.

After studies in Argentina and Italy, where he earned a master's in viticulture and oenology from the University of Bologna, the rugby-playing, landscape-painting, motorcycle-riding Santamaria moved to Texas. There, the Renaissance South American became the winemaker at Dry Comal Creek Vineyards and Winery in New Braunfels.

Meanwhile, he found time to begin developing wines under his own label. The next step came around harvest time in 2011, when he and his wife Angela opened their own establishment, adding an Argentine flair to the wines they make from Texas grapes.

Worth stopping for: See **Becker Vineyards** listing, page 11, and **Kerrville Hills** listing, page 31.

Singing Water Vineyards

5 miles west of Comfort off Texas 27, From 27, south on Pankratz Road, then right on Mill Dam Road; drive 4 miles and look for sign on right.

316 Mill Dam Road, Comfort • 830-995-2246
www.singingwatervineyards.com
info@singingwatervineyards.com

Tastings, tours: Thu. Sat. 11 a.m.-6 p.m., Sun. noon-5 p.m.
Varieties: Merlot, Pinot Grigio, Sauvignon Blanc, Syrah and blends.

On the Guadalupe Valley Wine Trail and the Texas Hill Country Wine Trail, Singing Water was opened in 2005 by Julie and Dick Holmberg after years of selling their Merlot grapes to other Texas vintners. It has a barrel room, a porch and a deck perfect for picnic lunches overlooking Bruins Creek, a tributary of the Guadalupe River.

A century-old barn rescued from the Hill Country has been transformed into a tasting room on the grounds – 125 acres of wooded hills and pastures dotted with goats.

The Holmbergs' family and friends came together to help plant the first vines, and this custom of family and friends' helping to bring in the annual harvest continues. In response to increased demand, the family has planted a second vineyard with Syrah and Pinot Grigio.

The name "Singing Water," the couple says, describes the sound that fills the air as the waters of Bruins Creek cascade over the waterfall.

Worth stopping for/overnighting: See **Bending Branch** listing, page 16.

Sister Creek Vineyards
12 miles north of Boerne on FM 1376.

1142 Sisterdale Highway (Farm Road 1376), Sisterdale
830-324-6704
www.sistercreekvineyards.com • sistercreek@hctc.net

Tastings, tours: Mon.-Fri. 10 a.m.-5 p.m., Sat.-Sun. 10 a.m.-6 p.m.
Varieties: Cabernet Sauvignon blends, Chardonnay, Merlot, Muscat Canelli, Pinot Noir.

Betwixt Boerne and the fabled metropolis of Luckenbach, between the cypress-lined East and West Sister Creeks in the Texas Hill Country town of Sisterdale (pop. 25), Sister Creek Vineyards winery is housed in a restored 1885 cotton gin.

Now, instead of processing everyone's favorite fiber, Sister Creek crafts French varietals — Chardonnay, Pinot Noir, Cabernet Sauvignon blends and Merlot — following the winemaking techniques of Bordeaux and Burgundy. The resulting wines have done well in California wine competitions.

Sisterdale began as a community of "free-thinking" German immigrants known as the Latin Colonies. These settlers studied in Latin and disavowed organized religion. In 1988, a century and a half later, this winery was established not far from one believed to have been built by the early European settlers.

44

Sister Creek is on the Texas Hill Country Wineries and Guadalupe Valley wine trails.

Worth stopping for/overnighting: See **Rancho Ponte** listing, page 39, and **Bending Branch** listing, page 16.

Solaro Estate

About 20 miles west of Austin near Dripping Springs. From Austin, take U.S. 290W toward Johnson City. Turn right at Fitzhugh Road; after a couple of miles, bear slightly left to stay on Fitzhugh; then turn left at Silver Creek Road. The winery will be on the left.

13111 Silver Creek Road, Dripping Springs
832-660-8642 • www.solaroestate.com • info@solaroestate.com

Tastings, tours: Sun., Mon. and Thu. 11 a.m.-6 p.m., Fri.-Sat. 11 a.m.-7 p.m.

Varieties: Merlot, Tempranillo, Syrah and blends including Grenache, Mourvèdre and Sangiovese. The winery also sells Italian wines from Emilio Romagna, and its vineyards produce Barbera and Montepulciano grapes.

This winery-in-progress is situated above Barton Creek, making it one of the closest wine destinations to downtown Austin, at just a 25-minute drive. Its tasting pavilion overlooks Dripping Springs Vineyard and is adjacent to the owners' racing thoroughbred operation, offering fine vistas of the Hill Country, with covered outdoor seating at the foot of the vineyards.

The owners, whose family has cultivated the property since 1909, trace their roots back to Italy's Emilia-Romagna region, where their forebears first made wine in the early 1800s. Their wine-making motto: "Art in science."

They style their dry red wines after those made there, traveling to Italy frequently and periodically flying in a consultant from Italy. They also bring back wines from the Emilia-Romagna region to sell in their tasting pavilion.

Solaro maintains an ambitious calendar of special events that includes Kentucky Derby and Tour de France celebrations.

Worth stopping for: North of Dripping Springs, **Hamilton Pool Preserve**, a grotto-like natural pool crowned by a 50-foot waterfall, is a popular destination from Austin (call ahead for swimming conditions, 512-264-2740, www.co.travis.tx.us/tnr/parks/hamilton_pool.asp). Dripping Springs' proximity to Austin means a number of dining options that are a cut above the usual, including **Creek Road Café** (512-858-9459, www.creekroadcafe.com), the **Goodnight Diner** (512-858-0426, thegoodnightdiner.org and the little **Thyme and Dough bakery** (512-894-0001, www.

thymeanddough.com). **Pedernales Falls State Park**, in Blanco County east of Johnson City, offers camping, picnicking, hiking, river swimming, tubing, wading, mountain biking, fishing, bird-watching (830-868-7304).

Overnighting: Nearby **Juniper Hills Farm** (830-833-0910, www.juniperhillsfarm.com) offers upscale cabins, cooking classes, massages and other indulgences.

Spicewood Vineyards

Off Texas 71 near the Burnet County community of Spicewood, about 35 miles northwest of Austin. From Austin, take Texas 71 west to CR 408 and turn left (south), away from the lake. Go about 7/10 mile; turn right on the first road, CR 409. Drive 1 1/2 miles through the vineyard and take the left fork; winery parking is on the right.

1419 Burnet County Road 409, Spicewood • 830-693-5328
www.spicewoodvineyards.com • wines@spicewoodvineyards.com

Tastings, tours: Wed.-Sat. 10 a.m.-6 p.m., Sun. noon-5 p.m. and by appointment.
Varieties: Chardonnay, Grenache, Merlot, Riesling, Sauvignon Blanc, Semillon, Tempranillo, Touriga, Zinfandel, blush wines and blends.

West of Austin near Marble Falls, the original winery structure was built to resemble a 19th-century Hill Country home with a comfortable front porch. It opened for business in 1995.

A two-story, 5,000-square-foot winery building was added four years later, with a large tasting room on the upper level, the winemaking equipment on the first floor; underground is a 400-barrel cellar. A deep-porched event center accommodating more than 200 guests, with its own stream flowing by, completes the complex.

A covered pavilion and a water fountain grace the grounds, which include a shaded area for sipping wine and picnicking while taking in picture-post-card views of the vineyard and the surrounding Hill Country.

The Ron Yates family and winemaker Jeff Ivy carry on the estate-wine tradition begun by Edward and Madeleine Manigold, whose wines were award-winners from their first year.

On the Texas Hill Country Wineries trail, the winery hosts gourmet dinners, pig roasts and other events — including Shakespeare productions — throughout the year.

Worth stopping for: Spicewood is home to several art galleries, including the **Gallery at**

46

Spicewood, which features art, handcrafted gifts and custom furniture (512-484-4514, www.galleryatspicewood.com). Near Spicewood are two natural swimming holes beloved among many generations of Hill Country natives: **Krause Springs**, an endearingly old-fashioned swimming hole and campground with waterfalls, is open year 'round (830-693-4181, www.krausesprings.net). **Hamilton Pool Preserve**, a grotto-like pool crowned by a 50-foot waterfall, is a popular destination from Austin (call ahead for swimming conditions, 512-264-2740, www.co.travis.tx.us/tnr/parks/hamilton_pool.asp). **Cypress Valley Canopy Tours** offers the Hill Country version of zip-lining south of Spicewood at 1223 Paleface Ranch Road (512-264-8880, www.cypress-valley.com). Also see **Flat Creek Estate** listing, page 24.

Overnighting: See **Flat Creek Estate** listing, page 24.

Stone House Vineyard

Between Austin and Marble Falls north of Texas 71. From Austin, take Loop 1 S, head west on 71, turn right onto Paleface Ranch Road (1 1/2 miles west of the Pedernales River), right on Haynie Flat Road at the T junction, then three miles to the winery on the left.

24350 Haynie Flat Road, Spicewood • 512-264-9890
www.stonehousevineyard.com • info@stonehousevineyard.com

Tastings, tours: Thu.-Sun. noon-5 p.m. and by appointment.
Varieties: Norton (and a Norton port-style fortified wine), plus Cabernet Sauvignon, Chardonnay, Marsanne, Riesling (including a late-harvest), Shiraz, Tempranillo, tawny port-style fortified wine and blends from Australian grapes.

This winery released its first vintage in 2004 and immediately scored a big win at the Pacific Rim International Wine Competition, a gold and "best of class" for its Claros red. Subsequent years found Stone House garnering more prizes.

The winery is very much a blend of Texas, Australia and California. Its 6.5-acre vineyard, planted entirely in native American Norton grapes, sits on a bluff overlooking Lake Travis, which fans its grapes with moderating breezes. The estate's Norton grapes go into the Claros and the Scheming Beagles port-style fortified wine; grapes purchased from Australia, where winemaker Angela Moench has roots, are the basis of Stone House's various other wines, along with Napa Valley grapes.

On the Texas Hill Country Wineries trail, the winery schedules a variety of events, from yoga to fine dining; check its website for details.

Visitors can walk the grounds; visit the tasting room and winery, built with huge limestone blocks; or relax on the patio.

Worth stopping for/Overnighting: See **Flat Creek Estate** listing, page 24, and **Spicewood Vineyards** listing, page 46.

Tehuacana Creek Vineyards and Winery

East of Waco. From I-35, take Loop 340/Texas 6 Loop and drive east on Texas 6 toward Marlin; proceed about 3/4 mile past Tehuacana Creek to the second mailbox on the right.

6826 E. Texas 6, Waco • 254-875-2375
www.wacowinery.com • info@wacowinery.com

Tastings, tours: Mon.-Thu. noon-5 p.m., Fri. noon-6 p.m., Sat. 10 a.m.-6 p.m.; closed Sun. Tastings and tours free.
Varieties: Blanc du Bois, Norton, sherry, port-style fortified wine, cherry and honey dessert wine, blends.

Tehuacana (sounds like "To Walk In A") Creek is named after the native Tehuacana people who lived nearby, but the owners of this family-run winery are natives of Sweden.

Wine aficionados Ulf and Inga-Lill Westblom had dreamed of creating their own vineyard and winery before they moved from Missouri to Texas. They planted their first grapes at Tehuacana in 1997.

The Westbloms grow such New World native grapes as Norton (also known as Cynthiana), Blanc du Bois and Black Spanish (Lenoir); they produce a dry sherry, a port-style fortified wine and a honey-sweetened wine called mulsum, based on a recipe from ancient Rome.

They offer wine tasting classes, monthly wine dinners and other special events, including a Scandinavian midsummer festival with Swedish delicacies on offer. Light snacks, including cheeses and homemade breads, are sold at the tasting room.

Worth stopping for: Waco is home to such quintessential Texan attractions as the **Texas Ranger Museum** (254-750-8631, www.texasranger.org), the **Dr Pepper Museum** (254-757-1025, www.drpeppermuseum.com) and the **Texas Sports Hall of Fame** (254-756-1633, www.tsof.org), plus the attractive and shaded **Cameron Park Zoo** (254-750-8400, www.cameronparkzoo.com). The **Waco Mammoth Site** (254-750-7946) features a dig shelter and a walkway with an overhead view of mammoth bones.

Texas Hills Vineyard

1 mile east of Johnson City on RR 2766, the road to Pedernales State Park.

878 Ranch Road 2766, Johnson City • 830-868-2321
www.texashillsvineyard.com • wine@texashillsvineyard.com

Tastings, tours: Mon.-Thu. 10 a.m.-5 p.m., Fri.-Sat. 10 a.m.-6 p.m., Sun. noon-5 p.m.
Varieties: Barbera, Cabernet Franc, Cabernet Sauvignon, Muscat Blanc, Muscat Canelli, Pinot Grigio, Sangiovese, Roussanne, Syrah, Tempranillo, ruby port-style fortified wine, dry Sangiovese rosé and blends.

A mile east of Johnson City near Pedernales Falls State Park, former pharmacists Gary and Kathy Gilstrap planted 35 acres of vineyards way back in 1998. The couple, with son Dale Rassett, built an environmentally friendly winery with 2-foot-thick walls of rammed earth; they call their tasting room, also of rammed earth and cooled by water flowing through pipes under the floor, their "cave above the ground."

Specializing in Italian-style wines, Texas Hills was the first Texas winery to produce an estate Pinot Grigio. The Italian influence was inspired by the rolling hills and the soil, which reminded the Gilstraps of Tuscany. All their wines, the Gilstraps promise, are "wines to share with friends."

The Gilstraps craft wines with grapes from its own vineyards, from other Texas Hill Country vineyards and from top growers in the Texas High Plains.

The family encourages picnicking on the patio — local cheeses and crackers can be purchased in the tasting room — and browsing in the gift shop. Check the winery's website to find out about gourmet Italian dinners, wine club parties and other events on the grounds. It's on both the Fredericksburg Wine Road 290 and Texas Hill Country Wineries trails.

In 2008, Joel Stein of Time magazine online gave Texas Hills' Syrah an "excellent" rating, saying: "I'd want to sneak it into one of Texas' legendary barbecue joints to drink it with some brisket."

Worth stopping for: Lyndon B. Johnson National Historical Park comprises two parks, one in Johnson City, with a visitor center, Johnson's boyhood home and the Johnson Settlement, and the LBJ Ranch 14 miles west of Johnson City near Stonewall (830-868-7128, www.nps.gov/lyjo). Several lavender farms can be found near Johnson City (check http://www.johnsoncitytexaschamber.com/). **Pedernales Falls State Park,** in Blanco County east of Johnson City, offers camping, picnicking, hiking, river swimming, tubing, wading, mountain biking, fishing, birdwatching (830-868-7304). Texas Hills is within an easy drive of the Hill Country towns of **Stonewall, Luckenbach, Blanco and Marble Falls**.

Overnighting: Chantilly Lace Country Inn Bed & Breakfast has six acres of landscaped gardens in the heart of Johnson City (830-868-2676, www.chantillylacesoaps.com). Near Stonewall is **Rose Hill Manor**, a replica of an Old South plantation house with, a reputation for fine dining and a beautiful view of the Pedernales River Valley (830-644-2247, www.rose-hill.com).

Texas Legato

4.3 miles southwest of Lampasas: From U.S. 281, take FM 1478 (Naruna Road) west of Lampasas 4.3 miles, just west of Pillar Bluff Vineyard.

2935 Farm-to-Market Road 1478, Lampasas • 512-556-9600
www.texaslegato.com • info@texaslegato.com

Tastings, tours: Fri.-Sat. 10 a.m.-5 p.m.; Sun. 12:30-5 p.m.
Varieties: Cabernet Sauvignon, Chardonnay, Petite Sirah, blends both dry and sweet, red and white.

On 21 acres next-door to Lampasas' other winery, Pillar Bluff, Texas Legato is family-owned and -operated, making wines from Texas-grown grapes. It's on the Way Out Wineries and Texas Hill Country Wineries trails. *Legato* is Italian for legacy and a musical term for smooth and connected notes.

"Our desire is to create smooth and connected wines," its owners say. "Our *legato* for our children and grandchildren is founded on hard work, correct decisions and principles made with support from our family and friends."

Worth stopping for/overnighting: See **Pillar Bluff** listing, page 36.

Three Dudes (and a Dog) Winery

East of San Marcos near Martindale. From I-35, take exit 205 and go east 3 miles on Texas 80; turn right at Wolf Creek Ranch & RV Park on Old Martindale Road (CR 102).

125 Old Martindale Road, San Marcos • 512-392-5634
www.threedudeswinery.com • dudes@threedudeswinery.com

Tastings, tours: Daily noon-6 p.m.
Varieties: Chenin Blanc, Merlot, white Zinfandel, blends

The winery gets its name from the trio who designed and built it, Terry Alford, Jeff Felderhoff and Ron Pontiff. They chose the banks of the spring-fed San Marcos River in a remote corner of Wolf Creek Ranch for their winery, built on the grounds of the cattle operation's old quarters. Decks and a patio terrace overlook the river.

The "dudes" encourage visitors to explore the grounds and check out native flora, a hand-dug well lined with Mexican brick and a majestic old mesquite grove they call "Big Sticker."

They take a nontraditional approach to winemaking, producing Chenin Blanc, Merlot, a white Zinfandel and blends from Texas grapes. Their motto: "It takes a lot of beer to make good wine."

Behind every good winemaker is a good dog, and the Three Dudes' canine mascot is a Brittany spaniel named Fideaux, in homage to his French ancestry and the owners' Louisiana connections.

Worth stopping for: Texas State University's **Aquarena Center** in San Marcos has been giving glass-bottomed boat tours of Spring Lake since 1946; it's being transformed into an educational center, with the Texas Rivers Center exhibit hall, the Wetlands Floating Boardwalk and other educational nature attractions (512-245-7570, www.aquarena.txstate.edu/). The **San Marcos River** is a popular tubing destination; the local Lions Club rents tubes and provides a river taxi service back (512-396-5466).

Overnighting: San Marcos' **Crystal River Inn**, a Victorian inn and spa with 12 rooms in three buildings set amidst gardens, offers themed getaways and elaborate breakfasts (888-396-3739, www.crystalriverinn.com).

Torre di Pietra

Ten miles east of Fredericksburg on U.S. 290.
10915 E. U.S. Highway 290, Fredericksburg • 830-644-2829
www.texashillcountrywine.com • tdp@beecreek.net

Tastings, tours: Daily 11 a.m. 6 p.m. Tasting fee.
Varieties: Blanc du Bois, Cabernet Sauvignon, Chenin Blanc, Gewürztraminer, Malbec, Petite Sirah, Primitivo, Sangiovese, rosé, port-style fortified wines and blends.

Opened in 2004, this winery brings a Mediterranean verve to the traditional German flavor of Fredericksburg. Ken Maxwell, a chemist reared in Fort Worth, toiled in Austin's semiconductor industry before launching his second career as a winery owner.

The winery offers a piazza with covered patios for outdoor parties and events, often with live music on summer weekend nights. Bring your own picnic hamper and pick up a bottle or two of the winery's best.

The stone winery houses a gift shop and large tasting room and serves various trays of food to complement the vintages. Check its website for special events, including those sponsored by the Texas Hill Country Wineries and Fredericksburg Wine Road.

"Enjoy the music, do a little shopping, and come back again with friends," says Maxwell.

Worth stopping for/Overnighting: See **Becker Vineyards** listing, page 11.

Valley Mills Vineyards

About 12 miles west of Waco on Texas 6 just past Cedar Rock Parkway.

8532 Texas 6 N., Waco • 254-848-4343
www.valleymillsvineyards.com
valleymillsvineyards@yahoo.com

Tours, tastings: Thu.-Fri. 2-7 p.m., Sat. noon-7 p.m., Sun. noon-5 p.m. Fee.
Varieties: Tempranillo, Viognier, sweet Tempranillo rosé and blends.

Founded by two Waco-area physicians and their wives, Valley Mills is finding that southern European grapes thrive on the rocky hillsides northwest of Waco, even though a local tractor operator hired to prepare the soil insisted nothing would ever grow there.

All vineyard work must be done by hand, because the land is too steep for mechanization. But the limestone-rich earth and the good drainage helped the venture win medals the year it opened, 2010.

Tempranillo, especially, likes Bible-belt McLennan County terroir, the owners say. A late freeze in 2009 knocked out some vines, but the hardy Spanish varietal came back with secondary shoots and proved 80 percent fruitful. The grape also is drought-resistant, so what could be better for Central Texas? Oh, and it makes good wine.

The winery building had been a used-furniture store, then provided storage for a landscaper. Now its 2,000 square feet offer enough space for a tasting room and gift shop. Visitors often bring their own meals to accompany the premise-made wines, and the winery is available for special events and dinners.

The vineyard is several miles away; visits can be arranged on request.

Worth stopping for: See **Tehuacana Creek Vineyards and Winery** listing, page 48.

Vineyard at Florence

From I-35, 8.7 miles west of Jarrell on FM 487; winery gate is directly across from CR 232.

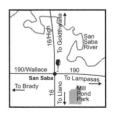

8711 W. Farm-to-Market Road 487, Florence
254-793-3114 or 254-793-3363
www.thevineyardatflorence.com • info@thevineyardatflorence.com

Tastings, tours: Villa Firenze tastings Thu.-Sat. noon-9 p.m., Sun. noon-6 p.m.; Bissinger's Chocolate Experience and Café Thu.-Sat. 11 a.m.-7 p.m., Sun. 11 a.m.-5 p.m. (hours may vary seasonally). Inwood Estates Winery Fri.-Sun. noon-6 p.m.; by appointment other days.
Varieties: Blanc du Bois, Cabernet Sauvignon, Lenoir (Black Spanish), Norton, dessert wine, blends.

There are actually two wineries within this upscale private residential community of Tuscan-style villas 45 miles from Austin, and noted winemaker Dan Gatlin makes wines — including some estate wines — for both.

The 600-acre development opened in October 2008 with a 30-acre vineyard, a winery and polo facilities; since then Gatlin has shifted some of the production of Dallas-based Inwood Estates to the Florence site. Both the Villa Firenze Winery and the Inwood Estates Winery are open to the public.

The winery building, overlooking gardens and the polo field, houses a tasting room, event facilities, an art gallery, a spa and a café and wine bar. There's frequent live music as well.

The Inwood tasting room, open Fridays-Sundays, is housed in the Italian Barn.

Overnighting: The Vineyard at Florence offers limited guest accommodations in its luxury villas.

Wedding Oak Winery

At the intersection of U.S. 190 and Texas 16 (Wallace and High streets) in San Saba, about 90 miles north of Austin.

316 E. Wallace St., San Saba • 325-372-4040
www.weddingoakwinery.com • info@weddingoakwinery.com

Tastings, tours: Tastings Wed.-Sat. 11 a.m.-6 p.m., Sun. noon-6 p.m.; fee. Tours by appointment.
Varieties: Sangiovese, Viognier, blush wine and red and white blends including Chenin Blanc, Cabernet Sauvignon,

Mourvèdre, Muscat Canelli, Orange Muscat, Pinot Grigio, Ruby Cabernet, Tempranillo, Trebbiano, Vermentino.

Travelers coming upon the unexpected charm of small-town San Saba, with its placid spring-fed duck pond and the rushing waters of its mossy, ferny little waterfall edged in bright cannas, will deem the charms of the northern fringes of the Hill Country every bit the equal of the more touristed areas farther south.

Wedding Oak is the town's first winery, occupying a renovated 1926 stone building right at the corner of the two main roads in and out of town and a block from the courthouse. After a decade of growing grapes for Alamosa Wine Cellars in nearby Bend, Mike McHenry put together a partnership to make his own wine. The winery he helms is named for a centuries-old live oak just west of town that local legend says has presided over romantic meetings and vows going back to Indian days.

McHenry, who has built a 7,800-square-foot, 10,000-case-capacity production facility next to the tasting room, turned first to Lubbock legend Kim McPherson to make his wines and now has brought in Texas viticulture maven Penny S. Adams as winemaker. She's working with grapes from McHenry's 9 acres, from other Hill Country growers and from Texas' High Plains.

Both snacks and gifts are available at Wedding Oak, which is on the Way Out Wineries and Top of the Hill Country wine trails. The winery's European-style courtyard is available for sipping and picnicking — as are the gazebo and grounds of nearby Mill Pond Park a few blocks away.

Worth stopping for: Mill Pond Park's pond, waterfall and streams offer a sweet little oasis in the heat of summer; on its 71 acres are the original mill house, the San Saba County Historical Museum, a nicely landscaped swimming pool, trails, sports fields and even an RV park. On the east side of town, the more old-fashioned **Risien Park** hugs the San Saba River next to the **LCRA Nature Park** (www.sansabatexas.com). Come October, it's the site of the **San Saba River Pecan Jam**, with music (Asleep at the Wheel headlined the first year), wine, food and more (www.pecanjam.com). Known for the pecans that grow in the sandy bottoms of the San Saba River, San Saba offers a half-dozen **pecan shops** (www.sansabatexas.com/pecans.htm) selling nuts and confections. And you can't miss **Harry's Boots**, a venerable Western-wear mecca occupying five landmark buildings across from the winery (325-372-3636, www.harrysboots.com). Looking for the **Wedding Oak** itself? Check http://famoustreesoftexas.tamu.edu/TreeHistory.aspx?TreeName=Matrimonial%20Oak.

Also see listing for **Alamosa Wine Cellars**, page 10.

Westcave Cellars Winery

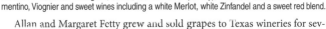

From Austin, take Texas 71 west to FM 3238 (Hamilton Pool Road); go west (slight left) and continue about 15 miles on Hamilton Pool Road to the winery, 2 miles past Hamilton Pool Park.

25711 Hamilton Pool Road, Round Mountain
512-431-1403
www.westcavecellars.com • info@westcavecellars.com

Tastings, tours: Fri.-Sat. 10 a.m.-6 p.m., Sun. noon-6 p.m.; Mon.-Thu. by appointment. Fee. Private tastings and tours by appointment.

Varieties: Cabernet Sauvignon, Merlot, Muscat Blanc (off-dry), Tannat, a limited amount of Vermentino, Viognier and sweet wines including a white Merlot, white Zinfandel and a sweet red blend.

Allan and Margaret Fetty grew and sold grapes to Texas wineries for several years before taking "a leap of faith" to open their own winery. Allan left the high-tech game for the different challenges of being a winemaker, and they opened Westcave in 2010.

The vineyards, about 7 acres of them, are a prominent feature of their property — they're open for visitors to wander, and Allan conducts private vineyard tour by appointment. The substantial tasting room, of Texas limestone, opens to merlot-hued Venetian plaster walls and a striking bar of granite and gold-leafed iron built by Fredericksburg stone and metal worker Phil Jackson.

"We try to do everything as local as we can," says Margaret, including wine labels by Texas artist Tim Wooding. Their wines are made from Texas grapes, too – some from estate grapes and some from High Plains vineyards.

Picnicking is encouraged, with a large covered picnic area set aside near the vineyard, and so is lounging in the hammock.

The Fettys are from North Carolina, and every couple of months they throw an authentic pig roast, bringing in a band for the party.

Worth stopping for/Overnighting: Practically next-door to the winery is **Hamilton Pool Preserve**, a grotto-like natural pool on the Pedernales River crowned by a 50-foot waterfall. It's a popular destination from Austin (call ahead for swimming conditions, 512-264-2740, www.co.travis.tx.us/tnr/parks/hamilton_pool.asp). **Pedernales Falls State Park,** in Blanco County east of Johnson City, offers camping, picnicking, hiking, river swimming, tubing, wading, mountain biking, fishing, bird-watching (830-868-7304, http://www.tpwd.state.tx.us/spdest/findadest/parks/pedernales_falls/). Also see **Bell Springs** listings, page 15; **Spicewood Vineyards** listing, page 46; and **Flat Creek Estate** listing, page 24.

William Chris Vineyards

On U.S. 290 between Stonewall and Johnson City.

10352 U.S. 290, Hye • 830-998-7654
www.williamchriswines.com • info@williamchriswines.com

Tours, tastings: Mon.-Wed. 10 a.m.-5 p.m., Thu.-Sat. 10 a.m.-6 p.m., Sun. noon-5 p.m. and by appointment; tasting fee.
Varieties: Muscat Canelli, Orange Muscat, Semillon, blends.

"Enchanté, y'all!" exclaims this sustainable winery that uses only Texas fruit, grown at vineyards it manages or from "personal friends" in the Texas industry, with a minimum of sulfates. Though relatively new, William Chris is already attracting attention in the Texas wine world.

Founded in 2009 by Bill Blackmon and Chris Brundrett, the winery employs small-batch fermentation and old-world techniques that visitors can watch.

Gourmet cheese plates are available in the century-old farmhouse that serves as a tasting room, and there's live music most Saturdays. With notice, the crew can provide picnic lunches.

William Chris is on both the Fredericksburg Wine Road 290 and the Texas Hill Country wine trails.

Worth stopping for/overnighting: See **Texas Hills Vineyard** listing, page 49.

Wimberley Valley Wines

Driftwood and Spring.

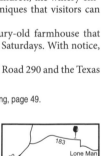

2825 Lone Man Mountain Road, Driftwood
512-847-2592 • www.wimberleyvalleywinery.com
wvvtr@yahoo.com

Tasting, tours: Daily 10 a.m.-6 p.m.
Tasting room: Old Town Spring, 206 Main St., Spring, north of Houston; Tue.-Fri. 11 a.m.-5:30 p.m., Sat. 10 a.m.-6 p.m., Sun. 1-5:30 p.m.; 281-350-8801.
Varieties: Viognier, blended whites and reds, including sweet wines, sangria and spiced varieties; fruit wines.

Between Wimberley and Driftwood among century-old live oaks, Wimberley Valley has undergone several renovations and expansions since 1983, making wine from grapes grown in Lubbock and Fort Stockton.

After fermenting, aging and bottling, the wines are shipped to the winery's tasting room in Old Town Spring, north of Houston, as well as to 250 other Texas retail outlets.

Wimberley Valley opened the tasting room because the winery was in a "dry" precinct. The precinct went "wet" in 2008.

Worth stopping for: See **Bella Vista Cellars**, page 14, and **Driftwood Estate Winery,** page 19.

Woodrose Winery

14 miles east of Fredericksburg, south of U.S. 290 on Woodrose Lane.

662 Woodrose Lane, Stonewall • 830-644-2539
www.woodrosewinery.com • greatwines@woodrosewinery.com

Tastings, tours: Summer hours Mon.-Fri. 11 a.m.-6 p.m., Sat. 11 a.m.-7 p.m., Sun. noon-6 p.m.; winter hours Sun.-Mon. and Thu.-Fri. noon-5 p.m. (closed Tue.-Wed.), Sat. 11 a.m.-6 p.m.
Varieties: Blanc du Bois, Cabernet Sauvignon, Merlot, Muscat, Syrah, Zinfandel, rosés, tawny port-style fortified wine.

The winery planted its first vines in 2001 and released its first wine in September 2002. Set on 60 acres of live-oak-dotted meadows, its lodge with tasting room and multi-level 3,000-square-foot deck are available both for sipping and for special occasions. Cheese plates are available for nibbling.

Woodrose sources fruit not only from its own vineyard but from other highly regarded grape growers around the state. The winery is on the Texas Hill Country Wineries trail.

The winery, which dates back to 1999, when the first vines were planted, was purchased in 2005 by Mike Guillette.

The new owner told *Texas Cooking and Wine* magazine: "My goal is to create an environment where people who are learning about wine can come and feel comfortable about wine, the process and themselves."

Worth stopping for/overnighting: See **Becker Vineyards** listing, page 11.

Panhandle Plains & West Texas

Though Texas' High Plains region doesn't get the kind of wine day-trippers the Hill Country does, it's every bit as important — indeed, arguably more so — in the story of Texas winemaking. Anyone who's serious about Texas wines knows that a pilgrimage to the Lubbock area — the home to Llano Estacado, Cap*Rock, McPherson and Pheasant Ridge wineries — is a must.

The High Plains may not have the picturesqueness of the Hill Country, but it has the terroir, the people and the history — and it's got the grapes.

The father of Texas winemaking, Doc McPherson, hails from here, which is one of the reasons Texas Tech University, home of the Texas Wine Marketing Research Institute, offers a degree program in viticulture and enology. In 1976, at the dawn of modern winemaking in Texas, McPherson, a chemistry professor at Texas Tech, co-founded Llano Estacado Winery, which was to put Texas on the winemaking map nationally. His son, Kim McPherson, whose résumé also includes a stint as winemaker at Cap*Rock, carries on the tradition with McPherson Cellars in downtown Lubbock, where he makes highly respected wines from warm-climate Mediterranean varietals.

The High Plains region, it turns out, grows something besides cotton and peanuts and prairie dogs. With its hot days and cool nights, its sandy soil and its low humidity, it is a paradise for grapes. Many of Texas' better bottles, no matter where they are crafted, start with grapes from the High Plains. And if those grapes were grown by Neal Newsom, that bottle is almost guaranteed to be special.

You can't mention wine on the High Plains without talking about Newsom, the McPhersons *père et fil* and Bobby Cox, who founded the groundbreaking Pheasant Ridge Winery and now serves as a viticulturist and mentor for the growing ranks of farmers who are converting acreage from water-guzzling row crops to grapes. It's a win-win situation, because the demand for High Plains grapes always exceeds the supply.

Bar Z Wines

Less than a half-hour south of Amarillo off Interstate 27/U.S. 60W/U.S. 87S (formerly Route 66). From I-27/U.S. 60S, take exit 108 for FM 3331 toward Hunsley Road. Turn left onto FM 3331 and then left onto FM 1541/Washington Street. Winery entrance is on the left just south of the animal hospital.

19290 Farm Road 1541, Canyon • 806-733-2673, 806-488-2214
www.barzwines.com • barzwines@amaonline.com

Tours: By appointment only. Check website for events.

The family-operated Bar Z aims to use only grapes grown in the Texas High Plains Viticultural Area in which it is situated, employing French oak barrels for extended aging.

Though not open to the public, the winery hosts the occasional special event; books tours by appointment; and is available for corporate events, board meetings, catered dinners and parties, offering cozy nooks or a spacious room with a grand view of the canyon.

Cap*Rock Winery

East of U.S. 87 on Woodrow Road about 5 miles south of Lubbock.

408 E. Woodrow Road, Lubbock • 806-863-4452
www.caprockwinery.com • info@caprockwinery.com

Tasting, tours: Visitor center open Mon.-Sat. 10 a.m.-5 p.m.; tours on the hour and half-hour, starting at noon. Tasting fee.
Varieties: Cabernet Sauvignon, Chardonnay, Chenin Blanc, Grenache Rosé, Merlot, Orange Muscat, Pinot Noir, Rousanne, Tempranillo, Viognier, blush, blends.

Built in 1988 with distinctive architecture inspired by Spanish missions, this imposing winery features 40-foot ceilings and an impressive approach through manicured grounds.

Cap*Rock, founded in 1988 as Teysha Cellars, has survived through several changes of ownership. The venture emerged from bankruptcy in 2010 when San Antonio entrepreneurs Jim and Cathy Bodenstedt made a winning $2.5 million bid.

It has been one of the gems of the High Plains wine region, having won a plethora of awards during its illustrious history, especially under the aegis of former winemaker Kim McPherson. In the seventh edition of his *Parker's Wine Buyer's Guide*, Robert Parker included Cap*Rock among only six wineries in Texas worthy of his mention.

This handsome winery is a popular site for special occasions. Check its website for events, including wine-and-food pairing classes.

Worth stopping for: Lubbock makes much of native son Buddy Holly, and fans of Holly and Texas music will want to visit the **Buddy Holly Center**, which also houses the **Texas Musicians Hall of Fame** and the **Lubbock Fine Arts Gallery** (806-775-3560, www.buddyhollycenter.org). They're in downtown's **Depot Entertainment District**, which has quite a hopping little nightlife and gallery scene (www.visitlubbock.org). There's also the massive **Buddy Holly Statue** and **West Texas Walk of Fame**, in the new **Buddy and Maria Elena Holly Park** (806-767-2241, www.visitlubbock.org). **Lubbock's National Ranching Heritage Center**, on the Texas Tech campus, showcases ranch structures in its 30-acre historical park and pioneer artifacts and art in its museum (806-742-0498, www.depts.ttu.edu/ranchhc/). The 248-acre **Mackenzie State Park**, within Lubbock's city limits, offers a golf course, amusement park and sculpture garden, but its signature attraction is **Prairie Dog Town** (806-775-2687, www.parks.ci.lubbock.tx.us). Lubbock also offers a hands-on museum and Omni theater at the **Science Spectrum**, (806-745-6299, www.sciencespectrum.com); for windmill buffs, there's **Lubbock's American Wind Power Center** (806-747-8734, www.windmill.com).

Overnighting: In Lubbock, the purpose-built **Woodrow House Bed & Breakfast** offers 10 themed rooms — including a caboose — with a pool across the street from Texas Tech (806-793-3330, 800-687-5236, www.woodrowhouse.com) The family of consummate High Plains grape grower Neal Newsom runs the **Rock'n-N Bed & Breakfast**, a circa-1914 ranch house on the plains near Plains, in Yoakum County near the New Mexico state line. Guests can book tours of Newsom's nearby vineyard (806-456-6877, www.newsomvineyards.com).

Christoval Vineyards

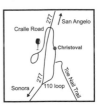

West of U.S. 277 15 miles south of San Angelo. From San Angelo, take U.S. 87S or Loop 306 and merge onto U.S. 277S toward Eldorado. Continue on U.S. 277S for 15.4 miles and exit right onto Cralle Road. From Sonora, go north on U.S. 277 from Interstate 10 for 45.5 miles; after crossing the Concho River, turn left onto Cralle Road.

5000 Cralle Road, Christoval • 325-315-8077
www.christovalvineyards.com • info@christovalvineyards.com

Tastings, tours: Thu.-Sun. 11:30 a.m.-6:30 p.m.
Varieties: Cabernet Sauvignon, Chardonnay, port-style Merlot, Riesling, Syrah, Tempranillo, Viognier, rosé, sparkling almond.

This West Texas winery opened in late 2010 alongside a 25-acre vineyard that dates from 1985.

Built amid stands of live oak and pecan near the banks of the Concho River, Christoval's 3,000-square-foot tasting room and event center is modeled after a 17th-century French chateau, with three tree-shaded patios, a fountain, a pergola and a catering kitchen for private celebrations and wine-club events.

Christoval makes wine from southern European grape varietals under the Christoval and Rambouillet labels.

Worth stopping for: San Angelo's **River Beautification Project** has brought a river walk and plaza, gardens, water displays, a performance stage, a playground, a visitor center and a nine-hole golf course to the banks of the Concho River in downtown San Angelo (www.sanangelo.org/goodtimes/attractions.php). **Civic League Park** is home to the **International Water Lily Garden**, with hundreds of water lilies blooming from spring through October, and the **San Angelo Rose Garden**. Open for visitors on Saturdays, the **Railway Museum of San Angelo** occupies the restored 1909 Orient-Santa Fe Depot (325-486-2140, www.railwaymuseumsanangelo.homestead. com). A **free-tail bat colony** shelters on the underside of the bridge at the Foster Road overpass at Loop 306 in San Angelo between late March and early November, and observers can see them emerge at sunset (www.sanangelo.org/goodtimes/attractions.php).

The 501 Winery

Three blocks south of the courthouse in downtown Childress.

204 Commerce St., Childress • 940-937-8155
www.501winery.com • bishoplonghorns@hotmail.com

Tastings, tours: Tue.-Sat. 10:30 a.m.-5:30 p.m.; tours by appointment.

This winemaking venture is named for the 501 Steam Engine used by the Fort Worth and Denver Railway (nicknamed "the Denver Road"). You can see the engine when you visit the winery. Winemaker — and Longhorn cattleman — Adam Bishop grows grapes at his vineyard on the plains; for the time being, his fruit is turned into wine at the Wichita Falls Vineyards & Winery, then sold, along with Wichita Falls' own wine, at 501's store in downtown Childress.

Llano Estacado Winery

3.2 miles east of U.S. 87S on FM 1585.

3426 E. Farm Road 1585, Lubbock
806-745 2258, 800-634-3854
www.llanowine.com • info@llanowine.com

Tastings, tours: Mon.-Sat. 10 a.m.-5 p.m., Sun. noon-5 p.m. Tastings free. Free tours with tastings every half-hour; last tour starts at 4; groups of 10 or more by appointment.
Varieties: Cabernet Sauvignon, Chardonnay, Chenin Blanc, Gewürztraminer, Malvasia Bianca, Merlot, Montepulciano, Moscato, Pinot Grigio, Sangiovese, Sauvignon Blanc, Tempranillo, Viognier, port and various blends.

Set in Buddy Holly country, originally better known for prairie dogs, cotton-growing and Texas Tech, this winery originally launched by two Tech professors in 1976 put Texas wine on the national map and proved that respectable wine can be produced in the Lone Star State.

The highest-profile and largest of Texas' boutique wineries, Llano Estacado has positioned its wines in more than 20 states and in seven countries in Asia and Europe. Llano Estacado vintages have been served at the White House under the two most recent Texas presidents.

The vineyards are planted at an elevation of 3,200 feet on the Texas High Plains. The grapes mature during warm days and cool nights similar to those of French growing regions. Llano Estacado uses grapes from its own vineyard; from surrounding High Plains vineyards; and occasionally, when demand exceeds supply, from outside Texas.

Llano Estacado shook up the California wine establishment when its 1984 Chardonnay snared a double gold (for unanimous decision) at the 1986 San Francisco Fair competition, the nation's prestige event. That and succeeding prizes have built a loyal following for its premium vintages. Llano Estacado lured winemaker Greg Bruni from California in 1993 to continue the tradition. Bruni is now vice president and executive winemaker, with Chris Hull, who came to Llano Estacado from Texas Tech, as winemaker.

Worth stopping for/overnighting: See **Cap*Rock Winery** listing, page 59.

McPherson Cellars

At the corner of 17th and Texas in Lubbock's Depot Entertainment District.

1615 Texas Ave., Lubbock • 806-687 9463 (WINE)
www.mcphersoncellars.com • info@mcphersoncellars.com

Tastings, tours: Mon.-Sat. 11 a.m.-7 p.m. Tasting fee.
Varieties: Albariño, Cabernet Sauvignon, Pinot Grigio, Rosé of Syrah, Roussanne, Sangiovese, Viognier, sherry and blends.

"Texas wine legend Kim McPherson is transforming downtown Lubbock's old Coca-Cola bottling plant into a showplace winery, with a bamboo-lined courtyard, fountain and patio, glass-block windows, a tasting room that can be viewed through the long window that used to frame the bottling line, a wedding chapel, an event center, an art gallery, a kitchen and sherry soleras on the roof," noted a *Fort Worth Star-Telegram* article by one of the co-authors of this volume.

Winemaker owner McPherson's name is synonymous with quality wine in Texas. His wines have won more than 400 medals for his former employers in the area — including two double golds at the San Francisco Wine Fair for Llano Estacado — before he struck out on his own in 2008. His new venture got an immediate nod from wine mikado Robert Parker, being named in the seventh edition of *Parker's Wine Buyer's Guide* as among only six Texas wineries particularly worthy of note.

Believing in the importance of "planting to the land," McPherson focuses on Rhone and Italian varietals, which he feels best suit his region. His aim is to make "wines of distinction with an Old World feel and character" — and at a reasonable price. His Sangiovese; his Tre Colore, a Rhone-style red blend of Carignan, Mourvèdre and Viognier; and his DBS, an Italian-style blend of Dolcetto, Barbera and Sangiovese, are among the most consistent and successful of any Texas wines.

"I wanted a place where I could produce about 7,000 to 8,000 cases," McPherson told the *Lubbock Avalanche Journal*. "I also knew I didn't want to do it far from Lubbock and out in the county."

So McPherson found a spot in Lubbock's Depot Entertainment District, where he hosts live music and participates in the district's First Friday art and gallery walks. The distinctively restored 1930s-vintage Coca-Cola bottling facility is hip, fun to visit and directly across the street from La Diosa Cellars, a charming wine bar with winery status operated by his wife, Sylvia. McPherson makes some exclusive wines for La Diosa, which also offers McPherson Cellars bottles and hosts live music at 901 17th St.

Worth stopping for/overnighting: See **Cap*Rock Winery** listing, page 59.

Mesa Vineyards

Formerly Ste. Genevieve Wines; 26 miles east of Fort Stockton off Interstate 10.

P. O. Box 697, Fort Stockton • 432-395-2417

Tastings, tours: None.
Varieties: Cabernet Sauvignon, Chardonnay, Gamay, Merlot, Pinot Noir, Sauvignon Blanc.

Texas' largest winery almost since its inception in 1987 as Ste. Genevieve, Mesa is situated near an 867-acre vineyard pioneered by the University of Texas Land Office. Aside from its cheap and moderately priced Ste. Genevieve wines, it produces a premium line, Peregrine Hill. Don't bother to visit, though — Mesa doesn't accommodate guests.

Pheasant Ridge Winery

North of Lubbock near the hamlet of New Deal. From Lubbock, go north on Interstate 27N and take exit 14; turn right on CR5600/FM1729 and travel east 2 miles; turn south at winery sign and go 1 mile to find winery on the left.

3507 E. County Road 5700, Lubbock • 806-746-6033
www.pheasantridgewinery.com • billgipson@aol.com

Tasting, tours: Fri.-Sat. noon-6 p.m., Sun. 1-5 p.m. and by appointment; tours and tastings free.
Varieties: Cabernet Sauvignon, Chardonnay, Chenin Blanc, Merlot, Pinot Noir, blends.

Just north of Lubbock in the farming community of New Deal, Pheasant Ridge was named for the wild fowl often spotted around the vineyard. If Willie Nelson owned a winery, it might look like Pheasant Ridge, whose raffish charm telegraphs its authenticity. A stone's toss from the vineyard are picnic tables, a tasting room and an arbor.

Under the aegis of Bobby Cox — one of the legendary figures in Texas wine and now a top viticultural consultant — Pheasant Ridge was one of the High Plains' pioneering wineries, and one of the oldest in Texas. It's now owned by Bill Gipson, one of the original investors.

From vineyards planted in 1979, Pheasant Hill strives to make wines in the French style, using French varietals, including a truly dry Chenin Blanc. All its wine is barrel-aged and estate-bottled, meaning that only its own grapes are used.

Wine critic Robert Parker has written: "Pheasant Ridge Cabernet Sauvignon is big, bold, and complex and competitive in quality with anyone."

Worth stopping for/overnighting: See **Cap*Rock Winery** listing, page 59.

Seifert Cellars and Wild West Vines

About 65 miles east of San Angelo and west of Brownwood. From San Angelo, take U.S. 67 east and take U.S. 83 south. Turn east onto FM 1929 and go about 13 miles, until you see a sign for Concho Recreation Area. Turn left onto RR 11 and watch for signs for Seifert Cellars. In a mile, turn right onto CR 4763, a dirt road. In about a mile, the road will fork in several different directions; choose the road to the left of the brown PRIVATE ROAD sign and follow it to the winery entrance.

15051 Lake Ivie Drive, Millersview • 325-234-7272
www.seifertcellars.com
dew@centex.net or steveseifert@suddenlink.net

Varieties: Cabernet Sauvignon, Chardonnay, Syrah, dessert wines and blends.
Tastings, tours: Fri.-Sun. 2-6 p.m. and by appointment.

Next to O.H. Ivie Lake, between Brownwood and San Angelo on the verge of the High Plains, Seifert Cellars planted its first vines in 2005. The first planting was Lenoir, or Black Spanish, the grape brought over by Spanish missionaries in the 1600s; when those vines thrived, Cabernet Sauvignon, Viognier, Riesling, Syrah, Vermentino, Chenin Blanc and Tempranillo were added.

Seifert produces sweet wines tailored to Texas summer drinking, with names like Starlight, Sunset and Rain. Some dry wines are available, too.

Worth stopping for: The Colorado and Concho rivers flow into **O.H. Ivie Lake**, which offers three public recreation areas with boat ramps, camping and picnicking. Bass fishing is especially popular, with boat and cabin rentals available (www.tpwd.state.tx.us/fishboat/fish/recreational/lakes/o_h_ivie/).

Val Verde Winery

From San Antonio, take I-90 west into Del Rio. Turn left on Veterans' Boulevard and go over the bridge. The road will fork at the next stoplight; turn right onto Garfield. Turn left at the next stop light onto Pecan Street; proceed about 1.5 miles; then turn right on Qualia Drive.

100 Qualia Drive, Del Rio • 830-775-9714
www.valverdewinery.com

Tastings, tours: Mon.-Sat. 10 a.m.-5 p.m. Free.
Varieties: Cabernet Sauvignon, Chardonnay, Lenoir, Muscat Canelli, Pinot Noir, Sangiovese, Sauvignon Blanc, tawny port, blends

Situated near the Mexican border, Val Verde is Texas' oldest winery, established in 1883 by Italian immigrant Frank Qualia. Friends were so taken back then with the wine Qualia made from the native Lenoir grapes that he began selling his output.

During Prohibition, the venture survived by selling table grapes; afterward, Val Verde returned to winemaking, standing as the state's sole winery until the 1970s. It remains a family operation.

Today the winery is best known for its Don Luis Tawny Port, and for the non-union wild geese that do the weeding.

Worth stopping for: Lake Amistad, one of Texas' largest lakes, offers camping, waterskiing, wakeboarding and fishing (www.tpwd.state.tx.us/fishboat/fish/recreational/lakes/amistad/). The **Whitehead Memorial Museum** comprises a collection of historical buildings and folk art (830-774-7568, www.whiteheadmuseum.org). Just across the border is **Ciudad Acuña, Mexico**.

Zin Valle Vineyards

About 15 miles northwest of El Paso just inside the border with New Mexico. From El Paso, take Interstate 10 northwest to the Artcraft Road exit; at the light, turn left on Artcraft (Texas 178); drive 3 miles and turn right on Westside Drive (FM 260). At the second stop sign, turn left; curve right onto Texas 28; then go 3/4 mile to the winery on the left.

7315 Canutillo-La Union Road (Texas 28), Canutillo
915-877-4544 • www.zinvalle.com

Tastings, tours: Fri.-Mon. noon-5 p.m., Tue.-Thu. by appointment.
Varieties: Chianti, dry and sweet Gewürztraminer, Malvasia Bianca, Merlot, Pinot Noir, sweet Zinfandel (white and red); rosé, sparkling wine and dessert wines.

When Kathi and Vic Poulos opened this winery in 2004 in the Rio Grande Valley, their aim was to return the El Paso area — where Spanish priests started a vineyard way back in 1662 — "to its rightful place as a recognized quality winemaking region."

Their winery now falls within the Mesilla Valley Appellation, the official viticultural designation for a grape-growing region that lies almost entirely in New Mexico.

Their first vines, all Zinfandel, were planted in 2001 on an acre and a half of drip-irrigated land, followed in spring of 2004 with two acres of Malvasia and Gewürztraminer. Then the Southwestern-style winery was built, with a tasting room and covered porch where guests can sample the output.

Zin Valle imports and sells a couple of unusual Italian wines: Vin Santo di Montepulciano, a traditional white dessert wine, and sangue di guida, a sweet red sparkling wine.

The barrel room is available for private functions, and there's frequent free music on Sundays (check website).

Worth stopping for: El Paso is a mecca for hikers, rock-climbers, mountain bikers and birders, with the nearby **Hueco Tanks State Park & Historic Site**, notable for the Native American rock paintings found there (www.tpwd.state.tx.us/spdest/findadest/parks/hueco_tanks/), and the **Franklin Mountains State Park** (www.tpwd.state.tx.us/spdest/findadest/parks/franklin/), where the **Wyler Aerial Tramway** lifts riders to the summit of Ranger Peak, 5,632 feet above sea level. Mexican and Tex-Mex food abounds in El Paso, with perhaps the most celebrated source being the **H&H Car Wash and Coffee Shop** (915-533-1144), whose weathered counter has attracted acolytes from far and wide, from roadfooders Jane and Michael Stern to the late Julia Child. Get your car hand-washed while scarfing down some stellar chiles rellenos.

North Central Texas

Stretching from the northern fringes of the Hill Country north to the Red River Valley, this region is full of variety, both in terrain — prairie, savanna, rolling hills, wooded areas — and in types of wineries.

It's home to the big Metroplex of Dallas and Fort Worth, where several urban-style wineries can be found, and from each city several outlying wineries are accessible for day trips.

At the northern edge of the Metroplex is the city of Grapevine, once a bucolic small town but now a high-traffic suburban community that aggressively markets its in-town wineries, tasting rooms, wine bars, restaurants and "wine train" to tourists. Grapevine hosts an annual series of popular wine-related events, including GrapeFest and the Lone Star International Wine Competition, and the Texas Wine & Grape Growers Association has its headquarters there.

Dr. Bobby Smith was one of the pioneers in the renaissance of the Texas wine industry in the early '70s with his La Buena Vida Vineyards in Springtown. Later wineries like Brennan in Comanche, LightCatcher near Fort Worth, Lone Oak in Burleson and the proudly green and sustainable Red Caboose near Meridian have drawn attention and become day-trip destinations.

A portion of the Texoma AVA lies in North Central Texas, which also boasts no fewer than six wine trails.

Arché

1 1/2 hours north of the Dallas-Fort Worth area off FM 677. From I-35 at Gainesville, take U.S. 82 22 miles west to Saint Jo; go north on FM 677 about 6 miles; right on Wagner Road.

228 Wagner Road, Saint Jo • 214-908-9055 or 214-536-6330
http://archewines.com/ • GoodWines@ArcheWines.com

Tastings, tours: Thu.-Fri. noon-7:30 p.m., Sat. 11 a.m.-7:30 p.m., Sun. noon-5 p.m.
Varieties: Cabernet Sauvignon, Merlot, Roussanne, Syrah and blends.

In Greek, "arche" means "beginning"; at this Red River Valley winery, Arché gets an accent mark and is pronounced *ar-KAY*. Among the smallest operations in Texas, Arché is dedicated to making big reds from its own Oak Creek Vineyards' Syrah, Cabernet Sauvignon, Mourvèdre, Merlot, Roussane and Carignan grapes.

Near the Oklahoma border, Arché is the northernmost winery on the CrossTimbers Wine Trail. Folks often combine a trip to Arché with a dinner at the neighboring Ancient Ovens (see below).

Worth stopping for: You'll sometimes see Arché owner Howard Davies working next door to the winery when **Ancient Ovens** is serving its five-course pizza-centered dinners from a massive brick oven. In fine weather, patrons can watch the sun set from the outdoor pavilion and overlook (BYOB; cash only; reservations essential at 940-366-4255). Nearby **Saint Jo**, once a stop on the Chisholm Trail, makes the most of its cowboy history, especially the **Texas Kings Hotel** and **Wild Horses Café** on the square (940-995-2565). The hotel can arrange for a golf outing at one of three nearby courses or, with advance notice, a trap-shooting session at the **Willawalla Creek Shooting Center**, run by Olympic champion Bret Erickson, where U.S. Olympic and U.S. Army shotgun teams train (706-577-1963; www.breterickson.com). Also on the square is **Trail Town Custom Leather** and **C.T. Chappell Boot Making School**, offering bespoke boots and boot-making classes (940-995-2600, www.trailtowncustomleather.com). **The Breaks at Bar H** (940-995-2309, www.barhbreaks.com) offers mountain biking on trails and track, with camping facilities, and **Red River Cycle Trails** hosts off-road motorcycling and four-wheeling along with camping, fishing and swimming (940-995-2903). **GermanFest**, at nearby **Muenster**, is held every April, with music, food and beer — some German, some Texan — and a scenic but challenging bike rally whose entry fee entitles one to free beer at the festival (940-759-2227, www.germanfest.net).

Barking Rocks Vineyard and Winery

About 40 miles southwest of Fort Worth off U.S. 377. From Fort Worth, take U.S. 377 southwest to Granbury, making a slight right turn on Business U.S. 377 north, slight right on East Pearl Street, right on North Houston Street, left on Lipan, right on Avery Road, left on Andrews Court, right on Allen Court.

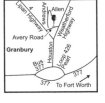

1919 Allen Court, Granbury • 817-579-0007
www.barkingrockswine.com • tiberia@barkingrockswine.com

Tastings, tours: Hours are elastic, but the winery is always open Sat. afternoons; also for special events such as First Friday concerts and by appointment; check website.

Varieties: Cabernet Sauvignon, Roussanne, Zinfandel, blends, strawberry.

Lawrence Tiberia, son of an Italian immigrant, gave up a "Gilbert"-like existence in a cubicle at a large utility company to devote himself to his true calling — making wine. (He also dropped his first name and a capital letter along the way, preferring to refer to himself as "tiberia.") He and his partner have been handcrafting small batches of wine in an old rock-walled barn since 2002, having sold their first vintage in 2004. He grows some of his grapes and sources others from Texas growers, including the High Plains' Bobby Newsom.

Barking Rocks' motto is "Making wine, friends and events happen"; the winery frequently hosts live music, including a First Friday Series. It's on the Way Out Wineries wine trail. Picnicking is encouraged, under shady trees on the 4.4-acre site, or on the converted barn's 80-foot-long porch.

Worth stopping for/Overnighting: Many B&Bs grace Granbury (www.granburytx.com), known for its eponymous lake and its picturesque courthouse square — lined with eateries, shops such as the delightful **Pan Handle** kitchen store (817-579-518) and the **Granbury Opera House**, a theater presenting white-bread live productions (817-573-9191, www.granburyoperahouse.net). There is a persistent myth that Lincoln assassin John Wilkes Booth escaped to Granbury, where he tended bar as "John St. Helen" in buildings on the square now housing the **Nutshell Eatery & Bakery** and **St. Helen's.** On the north end of town, **Niester's Restaurant & Deli** is a big friendly German-style restaurant that smokes its own meats and sells them, along with tempting baked goods, at a butcher counter up front. Great breakfasts; try the smoked pork chops (4426 E. U.S. 377, 817-573-0211).

Blue Ostrich Winery & Vineyard

Eight miles north of Saint Jo, between Denison and Wichita Falls on FM 2382.

5611 Farm-to-Market Road 2382, Saint Jo
940-995-3100 • www.blueostrich.net • Patrick@blueostrich.net

Tours, tastings: Thu.-Sat. noon-7 p.m., Sun. noon-5 p.m.; other days by appointment.

Varieties: Cabernet Sauvignon, Chenin Blanc, Merlot, Sangiovese, Syrah, Tempranillo, Viognier.

On a former ostrich farm, this venture opened in 2011 with a three-acre vineyard set against the hillsides of a working cattle ranch on the scenic Red River. Can't get more Texan than that.

The winery includes a tasting room and gift shop. And if you're in luck, an ostrich or two might be glimpsed on the grounds.

Worth stopping for: See **Arché** listing, page 68.

Bluff Dale Vineyards

Between Granbury and Stephenville, 2 1/2 miles north of U.S. 377 on CR 148.

5222 County Road 148, Bluff Dale • 254-728-3540
www.bluffdalevineyards.com • bluffdalevines@lipan.net

Tastings, tours: Mon. and Wed.-Sat., 11 a.m.-6 p.m.; Sun. noon-6 p.m. Tasting fee.
Varieties: Cabernet Sauvignon, Chardonnay, port-style fortified wine, sherry and red and white blends leaning toward the sweet.

Tucked away in the country, not too far from the Dallas-Fort Worth Metroplex, this rustic winery has been open since 2004 near the small town of Bluff Dale.

Owners David and Theresa Hayes invite you to enjoy their wines inside the large tasting room or on an expansive balcony to enjoy cooling breezes and views of nearby foothills.

Bluff Dale participates in Way Out Wineries events; check the winery website for live music and other special events.

Worth stopping for: Dinosaur Valley State Park, just northwest of nearby Glen Rose, contains some of the world's best-preserved dinosaur tracks. (Since the tracks are in the riverbed, they may not be visible if the river is high or muddy; check on conditions: 254-897-4588, www.tpwd. state.tx.us/park/dinosaur). Nearby is **Fossil Rim**, a drive-through exotic-animal park (254-897-2960; www.fossilrim.org). **Glen Rose** itself (www.glenrosetexas.net) is an interesting river town at confluence of the Paluxy and Brazos rivers. It was once a thriving recreation and health destination; a couple of the big old sanitaria are now inns, including the stately and serene **Inn on the River** (254-897-2929, www.innontheriver.com). And southwest of Glen Rose is the secluded, upscale-rustic **Rough Creek Lodge and Resort** (888-670-1223, http://roughcreek.com/), whose lauded dining room is open for reservations. In Stephenville, it sometimes seems most of the population of the surrounding counties — and all the motorcycles — are at **Hard Eight BBQ** at the intersection of U.S. 281 and 67 (254-968-5552, http://www.hardeightbbq.com/). Its fare is very similar to Llano's famous Cooper's, and we're told you can fly your jet into the Stephenville airport and take a golf cart to the Hard Eight. Also see **Barking Rocks** listing, page 69.
Overnighting: The winery's website has a list of more than a dozen B&Bs in the area.

Brennan Vineyards

From Fort Worth, take U.S. 377 south to Comanche; turn left on South Austin Street (Texas 16).

802 S. Austin St., Comanche • 325-356-9100
www.brennanvineyards.com • tina@brennanvineyards.com

Tastings, tours: Wed.-Fri. 11 a.m.-5 p.m., Sat.-Sun. noon-5 p.m., free tastings Fri.-Sun.
Varieties: Cabernet Sauvignon, Muscat Blanc, Syrah, Viognier (Brennan's signature varietal); a rosé and red and white blends, including Austin Street Three White Chicks – Semillon, Chardonnay and Viognier.

After practicing medicine for 30 years in Fort Worth, Pat Brennan was bitten by the winemaking bug and shelved retirement plans to launch a new career by building Comanche's only commercial winery. He and his wife found partners in the Wilkerson family, longtime publishers of the local paper, the *Comanche Chief*; the Wilkersons' son Lance became the vineyard manager. The Brennans' two children and their spouses also became part of the enterprise.

The winery opened for business in 2005 after two years of selling grapes from its vineyards to award-winning wineries, including Becker of Fredericksburg. Pat Brennan did the winemaking, with the help of consulting winemaker Kim McPherson of Lubbock; Brennan has since turned over the title of winemaker to Todd Webster. Together, they have made quite a name for Brennan wines — especially the viogniers — in a few short years. They make wine under two labels, Austin Street and their premium line, Brennan Vineyards.

Brennan has a picnic area near a creek bed as well as pecan and oak trees to contemplate before or after a tasting and tour. Though the estate vineyards are outside town — and Brennan sources some grapes from the High Plains — there's a small demonstration vineyard on the grounds.

The handsome tasting room was converted from the 1879 McCrary House, a limestone farmhouse. Nearby is the winery, made of stone and corrugated metal. Austin House is the events center, home to monthly wine dinners and available for functions. One of the stops on the Way Out Wineries trail, the tasting room offers gifts and wine accessories.

Brennan and McPherson, along with Gene Estes of Lone Oak Cellars, are behind the 4.0. tasting room just east of Fredericksburg (see listing on page 26).

Worth stopping for: Comanche County Historical Museum, open Thursdays and Saturdays, features a replica frontier store, blacksmith shop, filling station, barber shop and the Jack Wright Saloon, depicting gunslinger John Wesley Hardin's 1874 shooting of a deputy sheriff in Comanche (402 Moorman Road, 325-356-5115).

Brushy Creek Vineyards

1 mile north of Alvord, between Decatur and Bowie, off U.S. 287 on CR 2798.

572 County Road 2798, Alvord • 940-427-4747
www.brushycreekvineyards.com • brushyck@wf.net

Tastings, tours: Daily 10 a.m.-6 p.m. Group tours by appointment.
Varieties: Blanc du Bois, Cabernet Sauvignon, Chardonnay, Merlot, Ruby Cabernet, Sangiovese, Tannat, Tempranillo, ruby port, dry and sweet sparkling wine, dry and sweet red and blush blends.

Brushy Creek lies in the Cross Timbers eco-region, between the forests to the east and the plains to the west, about 50 miles northwest of Fort Worth. The vineyard was founded in 2002 by Les Constable, a retired nuclear engineer who had won awards as an amateur vintner.

In his Southwestern adobe-style winery built into the side of a hill, Constable has built a reputation for experimenting with varieties of grapes that are suited to North Texas' climate, such as the Spanish Tannat. He makes his wines exclusively from Texas grapes.

Wines from numerous other Texas wineries are for sale in Brushy Creek's gift and tasting shop, which is on the CrossTimbers Wine Trail.

Calais Winery

In the Deep Ellum district just east of downtown Dallas.

3000 Commerce St., Dallas • 214-453-2548
www.calaiswinery.com • bcs@calaiswinery.com

Tastings, tours: Wed.-Sun. 3-10 p.m. (hours curtailed during harvest in August; check website). Tasting fee.
Varieties: Cabernet Sauvignon, Muscat, Syrah, blends and a port-style dessert wine.

This urban winery was launched in September 2008 by an IT-exec-turned-winemaker named Benjamin Calais in Dallas' funky Deep Ellum entertainment district, a short cruise from downtown.

Its connection with the neighborhood is reflected in the names Calais has given his wines, honoring nearby streets. And the styles reflect his French birth: a Bordeaux claret style blend, an unoaked Chardonnay and a Cabernet-Syrah blend.

The tasting room also offers wines from other makers and countries.

"Each week we host a themed tasting of wines from a specific country along with wines from our own production," Calais says. "We thrive to make our tasting-room experience relaxed and educational." The tastings run Fridays and Saturdays; check the website for events.

Worth stopping for: **Deep Ellum** (a corruption of "deep Elm" Street, so called from the early-1900s days when it was a wide-open district of juke joints, blues clubs and other dens of iniquity; www.deepellumtexas.com) has long housed a lively entertainment scene, with numerous music clubs. Nearby downtown Dallas offers a vibrant arts district (www.thedallasartsdistrict.org), with the **Nasher Sculpture Center**, the **Crow Collection of Asian Art**, the **Dallas Museum of Art**, the **AT&T Performing Arts Center**, the **Winspear Opera House** and the **Morton H. Meyerson Symphony Center**. It's a short drive to the **Sixth Floor Museum** at Dealey Plaza, chronicling JFK's assassination and legacy (www.jfk.org).

Collin Oaks Winery

Southeast of Collin County Regional Airport five miles south of McKinney, just off FM 546. From Dallas, take U.S. 75 north, east on Eldorado Parkway, south on FM 546; follow FM 546 for 5 miles, then east on CR 398.

6874 County Road 398, Princeton • 214-504-9701
www.CollinOaksWinery.com • TheFolks@CollinOaksWinery.com

Tastings, tours: Sat. noon-5 p.m. or by appointment. Tasting fee (applied to purchase).
Varieties: Cabernet Sauvignon, Merlot, Zinfandel; rosé, semisweet and sweet blends; and specialty wines including blackberry, blueberry and hibiscus.

If sipping sweet wines in a country setting sounds appealing to you, it might be worth your while to find your way to this small, mostly family owned winery northeast of Dallas. Hibiscus wine, made from the tropical flower, is the big seller. You can also find Cabernet Sauvignon and other

North Central Texas

French varietals, but Collin Oaks specializes in sweet and semisweet wines.

"What we are really offering is what we call a 'wine and oak moment,' a feeling that only comes from the right combination of the personal touch, personalized wine and a place under an oak tree to enjoy them," the family says on its website.

Worth stopping for: McKinney's **Chestnut Square Historic Village** is a collection of 10 historic homes and buildings, stocked with period artifacts. It's open Tuesdays, Thursdays and Saturdays (315 S. Chestnut St., 972-562-8790, www.chestnutsquare.org).

CrossRoads Winery & Wine Bar

About 4 miles west of Dallas North Tollway on Frisco's Main Street (FM 720), which becomes King Road at FM 423.

15222 King Road, Suite 301, Frisco
972-294-4144 or 214-725-5646
www.crwinery.com • friscowinery@hotmail.com

Tastings, tours: Happy hour and live music Fri. 5-11 p.m. (reservations suggested), tastings Sat.-Sun. 1-6 p.m. Tasting fee.
Varieties: Cabernet Sauvignon, Chardonnay, Merlot, Sangiovese, Syrah; red, white and blush blends; white port-style fortified wine.

This winery moved from the town of Cross Roads in 2005 to a 3,000 square foot corrugated-metal warehouse when it was purchased by John Otis, a flight attendant who has made award-winning wines for more than a decade.

Otis buys grapes from West Texas for his wines. In 2008, one of his red blends won a double gold at Houston's big wine competition, reaffirming the fledgling venture's merits.

There's live music at the wine bar on Friday evenings and tastings on weekend afternoons, with appetizers to nosh on.

CrossRoads offers volunteers opportunities to bottle wine and stomp grapes — that's how Otis started out (check website for dates and send in your e-mail address). It's on the Munson Wine Trail.

Worth stopping for: Frisco is home to **Pizza Hut Park**, where the FC Dallas soccer team competes (www.pizzahutpark.com). Nearby is one of the state's few bicycle racing venues, **Superdrome** (www.superdrome.com).

Cross Timbers Winery

Downtown Grapevine.

805 N. Main St., Grapevine • 817-488-6789
www.crosstimberswinery.com
crosstimberswinery@directlink.net

Tasting, tours: Mon.-Sat. noon-5 p.m., Sun. 12:30-5 p.m.
Varieties: Cabernet Sauvignon, Chardonnay, Merlot, blush.

One of several wineries that draw tourists to Grapevine, Cross Timbers occupies one of the oldest houses in town, the 1874 Brock family farmhouse, with its white picket fence and balustraded porch. The owner, self-taught winemaker Don Bigby, says he bought the building without telling his wife, Penny. She knows now.

The Bigbys sell their own vintages, wines from other Grapevine producers and imported wines — including wine produced in Grapevine's sister cities, Parras, Mexico, and Krems, Austria. Deli meals are available on request.

Also on the grounds are a demonstration vineyard, a gazebo and a two-story party barn, which is available for special occasions.

Worth stopping for: Grapevine makes much of its wineries, vineyards and tasting rooms, with several wine-centric festivals throughout the year (www.grapevinetexasusa.com). Its quaintsy-posh **Main Street**, with cute boutiques and wine bars, is well worth a stroll. People love the **Grapevine Vintage Railroad**, whose 1896 steam locomotive pulls Victorian-era coaches between Grapevine's Cotton Belt Depot, 705 South Main St., and the Fort Worth Stockyards; tickets must be purchased in person on a first-come, first-served basis (817-410-8136). At **Grapevine Mills** mall, a popular attraction is the **LEGOland Discovery Center** (972-539-9360, www.legolanddiscoverycenter.com). For true Texas fare, try **Tolbert's** at 423 S. Main (817-421-4888).

Delaney Vineyards

In Grapevine just east of Texas 121; take Glade Road exit east, turn left on Champagne Boulevard and right on Merlot.

2000 Champagne Blvd., Grapevine • 817-481-5668
www.delaneyvineyards.com • info@delaneyvineyards.com

Tastings, tours: Mon. Sat. noon-5 p.m. Tours on the hour; tastings on the half-hour; fee for each.
Varieties: Chardonnay, Cynthiana (Norton), Muscat Canelli, Sauvignon Blanc; sparkling wine, rosé and blends.

Just off Texas 121 near DFW International Airport stands one of the state's most eye-catching wineries. Its slate roof, cathedral ceiling and stone masonry lend a European accent to this corner of North Texas: The winery was built to resemble an 18th-century French winery, with a grand 5,200-square-foot barrel room where the wine is aged in oak.

Delaney's finest can be enjoyed at the far end, where a tasting bar of Italian granite stands. Around the corner is a cute little gift shop.

The winery, among the most beautiful in Texas (and captured on our cover), is available for weddings and special events.

Delaney's main vineyards are in Lamesa, on the High Plains of West Texas, but the Grapevine facility has 10 acres of Cynthiana grapes. Founder Jerry Delaney has found Cynthiana, also known as Norton, to be well suited for the region's terroir, responding well to high humidity and hot summers.

Worth stopping for: See **Cross Timbers Winery** listing, page 76.

Enoch's Stomp Vineyard & Winery

About 30 minutes northeast of Longview: North on FM 2208, right on FM 449, left on FM 450, right at Ferguson Road; winery is on the left.

871 Ferguson Road (County Road 4312), Harleton
903-736-9494
www.enochsstomp.com • info@enochsstomp.com

Tastings, tours: Wed.-Thu. 10 a.m.-6 p.m., Fri.-Sat.; 10 a.m.-8 p.m.; Sun. noon-6 p.m. and by appointment.
Varieties: Blanc du Bois, Lenoir (Black Spanish), Norton Cynthiana.

Altus Koegelenberg, a fifth-generation grape-grower from South Africa, and Jon Kral, a physician from Washington state with theological leanings and a mission to found a retreat center, met at church and decided to combine ambitions.

The result is Enoch's Stomp, with Koegelenberg tending the vineyards and Kral using his chemistry background to create the wines. Their aim is to grow wine-producing grapes that thrive in the Harleton terroir while resisting vine diseases that afflict many Texas operations.

They launched their winery with 11 acres of vineyards on a former horse farm astride scenic hills. The barn became the winery. In 2007, two years after the vines were planted, the winery's '06 Blanc du Bois won two bronzes, two silvers and a gold medal at wine competitions around the country — not bad for a fledgling venture. In 2009, the '08 off-dry Blanc du Bois won Enoch's Stomp the Texas Vintner's Rising Star Award for young wineries from the Lone Star International Wine Competition in Grapevine.

The winery, a stop on the Piney Woods Wine Trail, is equipped to hold weddings and corporate events as well as group retreats. Lunch is served on Fridays and Saturdays.

Check out the Enoch's Stomp website. It's one of the best around, with a video interview of the partners. And it'll give you the lowdown on special events, some catered. Come by and see why these unlikely partners call it "Old World splendor in the most unexpected of places."

Worth stopping for: Jefferson, about 17 miles northeast of the winery on Big Cypress Bayou, boasts a remarkable collection of restored 19th-century homes transformed into B&Bs, along with home tours; antique shops; and tours via steam trains, horse-drawn carriage and riverboat (www.jeffersontx.com or www.jefferson-texas.com). About 30 miles east of the winery is the lush **Caddo Lake State Park**, with its bayous and sloughs, lodging in log cabins built by the Civilian Conservation Corps and a variety of outdoor activities. There are canoe rentals and pontoon boat tours daily except Wednesday (903-679-3351, www.tpwd.state.tx.us/spdest/findadest/parks/caddo_lake/).

Fuqua Winery

Near Dallas' Love field off Lemmon near Inwood, behind Home Depot.

3737 Atwell St., Suite 203, Dallas • 214-769-1147
www.fuquawinery.com • lee@fuquawinery.com

Tastings, tours: Wed.-Fri. 3-6 p.m., Sat.-Sun. noon-6 p.m.; call for Mon.-Tue. hours.
Varieties: Cabernet Franc, Cabernet Sauvignon, Chardonnay, Merlot, Syrah, Tempranillo, Zinfandel, blends.

Another new urban winery in Dallas, this one situated behind a Home Depot in a rock-walled light-industrial building, Fuqua hit the ground running by winning big at competitions a year after its tasting room opened in 2007 and went on to snag a double gold for his '06 Tempranillo in the prestigious San Francisco International Wine Competition in 2009.

Lee Foster Fuqua opened the winery with his wife Julia after running a helicopter charter service and computer networking business. He says this is a different kind of winery, making "serious wine for serious wine drinkers":

"Almost every winery in the United States is centered around a theme-park-type existence — weddings, bar mitzvahs, art shows, banquets, outdoor concerts, shows, etc., preoccupy everyone at the winery to the point where the quality of the wine suffers. On the other hand, wineries in Europe concentrate on making the best wine possible and focus noticeably less on the 'dog and pony show'. This is exactly what Fuqua Winery is all about."

Fuqua and Courtney Key share the winemaking duties; they use French oak barrels to make wine from Texas, California and foreign-sourced grapes.

Worth stopping for: See **Calais Winery** listing, page 73.

Grayson Hills Winery

About 50 miles north of Dallas east of U.S. 75. From Dallas, take exit 51 and turn right on FM 121/Stephens Street, then right on FM 121/TX 5/ Waco and left on FM 121/Jefferson. Continue on FM 121; turn left on FM 2729, right on Bub Hill Road and left on Ball Road.

2815 Ball Road, Whitewright • 903-627-0832
www.graysonhillswinery.com

Tastings, tours: Sat.-Sun. 1-6 p.m., weekdays by appointment.
Varieties: Cabernet Sauvignon; Tempranillo, port-style fortified wine, red and white blends both sweet and dry.

Some 45 minutes north of Dallas, this small winery and vineyard occupy 38 acres of rolling hills bordered by large oak and pecan trees. Rick and Connie Magers opened the winery in an old barn in 2005, five years after the vines were planted.

Calling it one of Texas' best-kept secrets, the Magerses consider their winery both a labor of love and a fun weekend destination on the Munson Wine Trail, saying: "Have a glass of wine in the loft, relax on the tasting deck, enjoy a picnic in one of the gardens or just kick back in a hammock under the oaks."

Homestead Winery at Grapevine Tasting Room

See **Homestead Winery** listing in Northeast Texas, page 94.

Inwood Estates Vineyards

5 minutes west of downtown Dallas, behind the Anatole Hotel in the Design District.

1350 Manufacturing St., Suite 209, Dallas • 214-902-9452
www.inwoodwines.com • getinfo@inwoodwines.com

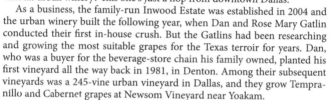

Tastings, tours: Sat. noon-5 p.m.
Varieties: Chardonnay, Tempranillo, port and blends.

Not feeling particularly outdoorsy? Hankering to visit an urban winery? This one's just a hop from downtown Dallas.

As a business, the family-run Inwood Estate was established in 2004 and the urban winery built the following year, when Dan and Rose Mary Gatlin conducted their first in-house crush. But the Gatlins had been researching and growing the most suitable grapes for the Texas terroir for years. Dan, who was a buyer for the beverage-store chain his family owned, planted his first vineyard all the way back in 1981, in Denton. Among their subsequent vineyards was a 245-vine urban vineyard in Dallas, and they grow Tempranillo and Cabernet grapes at Newsom Vineyard near Yoakam.

The Gatlins are proud of their wines, which are among the state's priciest and are found on the wine lists of numerous fine-dining restaurants around the state. They're known for their Tempranillo-Cabernet and a blend of Chardonnay and Palomino, a Spanish grape primarily used in making sherry. They've been recognized by no less a personage than Robert Parker, who named them among six Texas wineries worthy of notice in the seventh edition of his "Parker's Wine Buying Guide."

The Gatlins have three tiers of wine production: estate-level wines, all from Texas grapes; limited-production wines, all from Texas grapes; and "segundo," or second-level wines, from Texas and American grapes.

They also have a presence in the Hill Country, operating the Vineyard at Florence (see page 53) and selling their wines at the new Mendelbaum Cellars tasting room near Fredericksburg.

Worth stopping for: See **Calais Winery** listing, page 73.

La Buena Vida Vineyards

La Buena Vida Vineyards No. 1 at Springtown: 25 miles west of Fort Worth off Texas 199 just west of Springtown. Go south on Old Springtown Road for 3.4 miles; turn left on Mill Road for 3/4 mile and then right on Vineyard Lane.

650 Vineyard Lane, Springtown • 817-821-6794
www.crosstimberswinetrail.com/guest/lbv-springtown.html

Tastings, tours, sales: Sat. 10 a.m.-5 p.m., Sun. noon-5 p.m.; other times by appointment.
Varieties: Pinot Blanc, Pinot Grigio, Viognier, Tempranillo, port, honey-based mead, blends.

Dr. Bobby Smith established one of the oldest modern-era Texas wineries in 1972 when he founded an organic operation in Springtown. He christened his venture La Buena Vida ("The Good Life"), and it has brought much joy to regional drinkers and garnered a few prizes along the way.

His winery's grapes are grown in Springtown, then crushed for the winery's brands — La Buena Vida, Smith Estate and Walnut Creek Cellars. And he has added Nanie Bell Artisan Cheese Shoppe, named for his mother and offering semi-soft and soft varieties made on site.

Landon Winery

McKinney and Greenville.

www.landonwinery.com • winery@landonwinery.com
Landon Winery at McKinney: North of Dallas just east of U.S. 75, on the square in downtown McKinney off TX Spur 359 (Louisiana Street).

101 N. Kentucky St., McKinney • 972-542-3030
Landon Winery at Greenville: Northwest of Dallas in downtown Greenville at the intersection of U.S. 76 and U.S. 65 Business Route.

2508 Lee St., Greenville • 903-454-7878

Tastings, tours: Mon.-Thu. 11 a.m.-9 p.m.; Fri. 11 a.m.-11 p.m.; Sat. 10 a.m.-11 p.m.; Sun. noon -9 p.m.
Varieties: Amarone, Cabernet Sauvignon, Chardonnay, Merlot, Pinot Grigio, Pinot Noir, Riesling; rosé, dessert wines, sparkling wine, peach and raspberry wines.

These urban wineries showcase wines made by Bob Landon, who transferred the operation from a Kansas City basement to North Texas 15 years ago. His original winery, smack-dab in historic downtown McKinney, occupies a circa-1900 building with an old well in the barrel room; his second venture is in the old Kress Building in downtown Greenville. The Greenville winery serves as a production and distribution center with a tasting room, patio, educational vineyard, working well and irrigation tower.

Both have the same hours, both offer live music and special events on weekends (check website) and both are on the Munson Wine Trail. At Greenville, the latest addition is the City Bistro (903-454-4500), offering an Italian-leaning menu for lunch and dinner daily.

Worth stopping for: For McKinney, See **Collin Oaks Winery** listing, page 74.

LightCatcher Winery & Bistro

15 miles northwest of downtown Fort Worth, just outside Lake Worth. From TX 199 (Jacksboro Highway), turn west on Confederate Park Road and go 1.8 miles.

6925 Confederate Park Road, Fort Worth • 817-237-2626
www.lightcatcher.com • info@lightcatcher.com

Tastings, tours: Sun. and Wed. noon-6 p.m., Thu.-Sat. noon-9 p.m. Tasting fee.
Bistro: Lunch Fri.-Sun. noon-3 p.m. (until 6 on jazz Sundays); dinner Thu. 5:30-8:30 p.m., Fri.-Sat. 5:30-10 p.m.
Varieties: Cabernet Sauvignon, Chardonnay, Orange Muscat, Merlot, red and white blends, rosé; spiced wine, dessert wines and fortified wines.

This "micro-winery" is quite the success story in North Texas.

With its bucolic setting and expansive live-oak-shaded patio and arbor, LightCatcher offers a full schedule of events, including live jazz on the first and third Sundays of the month and new-vintage release parties.

The on-site kitchen supplies lunch Fridays through Sundays and ambitious dinner offerings Fridays and Saturdays; cheese plates are available through the week. In warm weather, Thursday is grill-out night. The winery houses an art gallery and sells gift baskets, stemware and local crafts.

Caris Turpen, a transplanted Californian and Emmy-winning cinematographer, always loved winemaking. She decided to make her ambition a reality when she moved to the Fort Worth area with her native-Texan husband, Terry. She began buying grapes from Texas' High Plains, and it didn't take long for her wines to begin garnering attention and awards.

Having quickly outgrown their original winery in Fort Worth, the Turpens relocated on four acres of live-oak groves, where in 2003 they built a tile-roofed, rock-walled Tuscan-style winery. Look for a meditation labyrinth, ponds and outdoor sculptures.

The building and grounds at LightCatcher, one of the stops on the Cross-Timbers Wine Trail, are available for special events.

Turpen calls winemaking "art and science stirred by mystery."

Worth stopping for: Fort Worth offers several popular and safe areas for visitors: **Sundance Square** (www.sundancesquare.com), a restored shopping, dining and entertainment district downtown, includes a pocket-sized gem, the **Sid Richardson Museum**, featuring a lode of Remington and Russell paintings (817-332-6554, www.sidrichardsonmuseum.org). The **Cultural District** on the near west side offers three architecturally significant art museums within walking distance of each other: the **Kimbell Art Museum** (817-332-8451, www.kimbellart.org), the **Amon Carter Museum of American Art** (817-738-1933, www.cartermuseum.org) and the **Modern Art Museum of Fort Worth** (817-738-9215, http://themodern.org). Also nearby: the **National Cowgirl Hall of Fame** (817-336-4475, www.cowgirl.net) and the **Fort Worth Museum of Science and History** (817-255-9300, www.fwmuseum.org), which includes the **Cattle Raisers Museum**. The **Historic Stockyards District** (www.fortworthstockyards.org), north of downtown, boasts rodeos, restaurants and dance halls, including **Billy Bob's Texas** (817-624-7117, www.billy bobstexas.com), known as the world's largest honky-tonk. The nifty **Stockyards Museum** (www.stockyardsmuseum.org) is housed in the iconic **Livestock Exchange Building**. A slick new dining, entertainment and retail district has evolved along and south of **West Seventh Street**, linking downtown with the Cultural District. And the historic **Fairmount** neighborhood (www.historicfairmount.com) just south of downtown boasts a local-centric restaurant row along Magnolia Avenue. Several blocks north is award-winning **Rahr & Sons Brewing Co.**, with an open house every Wednesday and Saturday (817-810-9266; www.rahrbrewing.com).

Lone Oak Vineyards

South of Fort Worth off I-35W. From I-35W in Burleson, take exit 37 for TX 174 (Wilshire Boulevard), then turn left on FM 731 (John Jones Drive).

2116 FM 731, Burleson • 817-426-6625
www.loneoakwinery.com • tastingroom@loneoakwinery.com

Tastings, tours: Thu.-Sat. noon-8 p.m. (may change seasonally). Tours by appointment. Tasting fee.
Varieties: Blanc du Bois, Merlot, Tempranillo, red blends; port- and Madeira-style fortified wines.

Relocated from Valley View in 2006, this winery on 52 scenic acres includes vines dating back to 1999.

They were planted by owner Gene Estes, a microbiologist by training who pursued his winemaking passion after a career in the pharmaceutical industry.

Estes inherited the previous owners' brands, assets, stock and consultant winemaker, ensuring continuity. One season he had to contend with invading feral pigs, which inspired a wine he named Hog Wild.

He uses estate-grown grapes and continues to buy grapes from the owners of the original vineyards in Valley View; he also buys some High Plains grapes from legendary grower Neal Newsom. The grapes are hand-picked and fermented in French oak barrels, then hand-bottled.

Shady picnic areas grace the grounds, which include a tasting room in the winery building. Look for live music on the occasional Friday or Sunday, as well as CrossTimbers Wine Trail events; box lunches are available with 48 hours' advance notice for your group.

Estes' latest endeavor is a partnership with the Brennan and McPherson wineries, opening 4.0 Cellars tasting room in the Hill Country (see page 26).

Worth stopping for: See **LightCatcher Winery** listing, page 82.

Rising Star Vineyards

See listing in **"Hill Country and Central Texas"** section, page 40.

San Martiño Winery & Vineyards

Northeast of Dallas and just east of Lake Ray Hubbard. From I-30, take the TX 205 exit north for about 4 miles; after crossing two small bridges, look for the winery 200 feet up the road on the left.

12515 Texas 205 N., Rockwall   •   972-722-6043
www.sanmartinowinery.com   •   winery@sanmartinowinery.com

Tastings, tours: Thu.-Sat. 1-9 p.m., Sun. 1-6 p.m., or by appointment. Fee. Group tasting tours with winemaker by advance reservation (fee).
Varieties: Cabernet Sauvignon, Chardonnay, Merlot, Petite Sirah, Petit Verdot, Sangiovese, Syrah, Tempranillo, Zinfandel and blends; late-harvest Zinfandel port-style fortified wine.

Convenient to Dallas, San Martiño is situated on eight acres near Lake Ray Hubbard. You can pack a basket and picnic on its umbrella-tabled outdoor patio or sip a variety of wines on the tree-shaded deck.

This North Texas winery is inspired by Spain's San Martiño, a Galician winemaking village where owner Emilio Ramos worked in the family vineyard. The UC-Davis-trained Ramos says he's borrowed the best techniques from Spain and California in his "ongoing search for bottled nirvana."

And he is off to a good start. Opening for business in 2004, San Martiño was named "best new winery" in 2005 by the Wine Society of Texas.

The tasting room includes a shop featuring imported crystal glassware, books and gift items. There's live music most Saturdays; on one Saturday a month, a paella feast is served (check website).

Sunset Winery

Just south of Fort Worth off I-35W. From the north, take Exit 35 south on the service road, cross the highway, turn left at the stop sign and left on CR 530B. From the south, take Exit 32, continue north on the service road for 2 miles and turn right on CR 530B.

1535 S. Burleson Blvd., Burleson • 817-426-1141
www.sunsetwinery.com • www.sunset.winery.mail@sbcglobal.net

Tastings, tours: Thu.-Sun. noon-7 p.m. and by appointment. Fee for tastings and tours.
Varieties: Cabernet Sauvignon, Malbec, Merlot, Orange Muscat, Pinot Gris; blends; dry and sweet açaí wines.

This winery was launched by Birgit and Bruce Anderson, who began selling wines in October 2005, becoming the first commercial winery in Johnson County.

But they began building their vineyard back in 1996, establishing it on the rural Burleson acre where they had raised their family while Bruce was a sociology professor at the University of Texas at Arlington. In 2003, they replaced Cabernet vines with disease-resistant Black Spanish. Meantime, they make wine with grapes from elsewhere in Texas. And here's something novel: Wine made from açaí (AH-sigh-ee), the South American palm fruit widely touted for antioxidant qualities.

"We produce limited quantities of premium, handcrafted wines," the Andersons say. "Our goal is to produce wines that we can proudly place on wine lists in the company of well known brands from around the world."

They host a happy hour with free munchies from 4 to 7 p.m. on Thursdays and Fridays, on the deck or in the barrel room. Other events include a seasonally themed multi-course dinner and "dinner and a movie" nights.

Worth stopping for: See **LightCatcher Winery** listing, page 82.

Texoma Winery

An hour northeast of Dallas between Sherman and Whitewright. From U.S. 75, take TX 121 toward Bonham, left on TX 160, left on FM 697, right on Judge Carr Road.

9 Judge Carr Road, Whitewright • 903-364-5242
www.texomawinery.com • info@texomawinery.com

Tastings, tours: Tastings Sun. afternoons by appointment; tours and bottle sales other days by appointment. Check website.
Varieties: Chenin Blanc, Merlot, Muscat Canelli, Viognier, red and white blends.

This family-owned winery just south of the Red River takes pride in producing wines to please the "Texas wine and beer drinker." Using mostly High Plains grapes, Texoma makes wines under the Texas Tasting and Whispering Willow labels, as well as winemaker Bob White's QuailTail, and sells wines from other Texas wineries. Texoma offers vineyard picnics, classes and private tastings; it's on the Munson Wine Trail.

Times Ten Cellars

Lakewood area of Dallas and near west side of Fort Worth.

www.timestencellars.com
kert@timestencellars.com

Times Ten Cellars Dallas
6324 Prospect Ave., Dallas
214-824-9463

Tastings: Mon. 5-10 p.m., Tue.-Wed. 1-10 p.m., Thu. 1-11 p.m., Fri.-Sat. 1 p.m.-midnight, Sun. 3-9 p.m.

Times Ten Cellars Fort Worth
1100 Foch St., Fort Worth • 817-336-9463

Tastings: Tue.-Wed. 1-10 p.m., Thu. 1-11 p.m., Fri. Sat. 1 p.m.-midnight, Sun. 3 9 p.m.
Varieties: Cabernet Sauvignon, Carignan, Chardonnay, Gewurztraminer, Grenache, Malbec,

North Central Texas

Merlot, Muscat Blanc, Petite Sirah, Pinot Grigio, Pinot Noir, Muscat Blanc, Sangiovese, Sauvignon Blanc, Syrah, Zinfandel, blends and rosé.

Times Ten Cellars is a full-production winery and friendly wine bar east of downtown Dallas, in the old Lakewood neighborhood post office, with a sibling Fort Worth winery in a former small factory building in the burgeoning, newly hip neighborhood between downtown and the cultural district to its west.

The operation uses grapes from California and from a sister vineyard in the West Texas town of Alpine. It also buys finished bulk wine and bottles it. At both wine bars, the Times Ten wine list is supplemented by select wines from other Texas makers. Times Ten also buys finished bulk wine from California and bottles it in Texas under its label.

Dallas-based wine critic Jeff Siegel (www.winecurmudgeon.com) writes: "The tasting room is quiet and tasteful, just the sort of place that appeals to its Gen X and baby-boomer customers."

Both wine bars host occasional live jazz and happy hours.

Worth stopping for: See **Calais Winery (Dallas)**, page 73, and **LightCatcher Winery (Fort Worth)**, page 82.

Triple R Ranch & Winery and Lone Star Wine Cellars

100 miles northwest of Dallas near the Red River, off U.S. 82 just east of Gainesville.

2276 County Road 125, Whitesboro
214-850-4020 or 940-665-4750
www.thetriplerranch.com • ronaldross@sbcglobal.net

Tours: By appointment.
Varieties: Cabernet Sauvignon, Chardonnay, Chenin Blanc, Gewürztraminer, Merlot, Riesling, Sangiovese, Shiraz, red blends and port-style fortified wine.

Tasting room: Lone Star Wine Cellars, 103 E. Virginia St., Suite 104, McKinney
972-547-9463
www.lonestarwinecellars.com

Hours: Tue.-Thu. 2-9 p.m., Fri. 1-11 p.m., Sat. 11 a.m.-11 p.m., Sun. 2-6 p.m.

Triple R is a scenic winery situated on a 100-acre, high-fenced exotic-game ranch. Graced with three miles of trails from which to observe deer and antelope, Triple R hosts high-rolling hunters for game and skeet shooting, archery, fishing and other manly stuff. In addition, the ranch is home to Arabian horses, Texas Longhorn cattle and a collection of domesticated fowl.

As might be expected for a game ranch, Triple R specializes in rich reserve and meritage-style wines, particularly reds. Winery tours are by appointment only, but you can taste the wines at Triple R's tasting room in downtown McKinney: Lone Star Wine Cellars, a joint venture of Triple R and Wales Manor Winery & Vineyard (see next entry).

Wales Manor Winery & Vineyard and Lone Star Wine Cellars

Northeast of McKinney off U.S. 75. Exit east on U.S. 380 (University Drive) and go 3 1/2 miles to FM 1827; turn left and go north about 2 miles to New Hope; turn right on CR 408; the winery is about 1 mile on the right.

Winery and vineyard: 4488 County Road 408, McKinney
972-542-0417 • www.walesmanor.com
winery@walesmanor.com

Tastings, tours: Spring/summer hours, noon-7 p.m. Sat.-Sun.; fall hours, noon-6 p.m.; open selected weekends in winter (call ahead). Tastings and tours free.
Varieties: Blanc du Bois, Cabernet Sauvignon, Merlot, Ruby Cabernet, blends.

Tasting room: Lone Star Wine Cellars, 103 E Virginia St., Suite 104, McKinney
972-547-9463 • www.lonestarwinecellars.com
Hours: Tue.-Thu. 2-9 p.m., Fri. 1-11 p.m., Sat. 11 a.m.-11 p.m., Sun. 2-6 p.m.

In a rural corner of Collin County north of Dallas, this winery with a 10,000-case capacity sits near a three-acre vineyard of Cabernet Sauvignon grapes.

The vineyard was established in 1999, began selling wines in 2003 and opened to the public in 2007 with an ambitious building program, offering free tastings on weekends. Now Wales Manor calls itself "The Best Little Winehouse in Texas."

Weekend visitors are urged to bring a picnic basket for the hilltop patio.

Of particular note is the ambitious singer/songwriter concert series hosted by Wales Manor (check website for schedule).

The winery showcases its wines in downtown McKinney in the Lone Star Wine Cellars tasting room.

Worth stopping for: See **Collin Oaks Winery** listing, page 74.

Weinhof Winery

Forestburg and Muenster.

www.WeinhofWinery.com
Brenda@weinhofwinery.com

Weinhof Winery of Forestburg: North of Fort Worth; from I-35 at Valley View, take FM 922 west 25 miles to Forestburg, at the intersection of farm roads 455, 677, 922 and 1655.

16678 Farm-to-Market Road 455, Forestburg • 940-964-2552

Tastings, tours: Sat.-Sun. noon-5 p.m. or by appointment; call for other hours.

Weinhof of Muenster tasting room: North of Fort Worth; from I-35 at Gainesville, take U.S. 82 west 13 miles to Muenster.

123 W. Division St. (U.S. 82), Muenster • 940-759-4637

Tastings: Summer hours Fri.-Sat. noon-7 p.m., Sun. noon-6 p.m.; winter hours Fri. 2-6 p.m., Sat. noon-6 p.m. (later for special events), Sun. noon-5 p.m., or by appointment.
Varieties: Blanc du Bois, Cabernet Sauvignon, Chardonnay, Merlot, Riesling, Sangiovese, Zinfandel; blush and sweet wines; various fruit wines, from persimmon to watermelon.

A small family-run operation with its production facility in Forestburg, Weinhof recently opened a German-style weinstube tasting room in Muenster, a town that makes the most of its Germanic heritage. Brenda Thompson, who is the winemaker, runs the venture with her husband, Larry, and together they work to blend Old World charm with Texas hospitality.

In Muenster, the Thompsons encourage visitors to pack a lunch — perhaps from the nearby Fischer's Meat Market, with its glockenspiel clock — and use the winery's picnic tables after sampling its diverse offerings of dry and sweet small-batch grape wines as well as an extensive line of fruit wines. Weinhof's specialty is wines handcrafted from locally grown peaches, pears, apples, plums, strawberries, blackberries — even watermelons and persimmons.

In the Red River Valley region, Weinhof is on the Red River Wine Trail.

Worth stopping for: Muenster's **GermanFest** is held every April, with music, food and beer — some German, some Texan. There's also a scenic but challenging bike rally whose entry fee entitles one to free beer at the festival (940-759-2227, www.germanfest.net).

Wichita Falls Vineyards & Winery

Just west of Wichita Falls near the Oklahoma border. From U.S. 287, take the Peterson Road exit and go south on Peterson Road South to the winery.

3399B Peterson Road S., Iowa Park
940-855-2093
www.wichitafallsvineyardsandwinery.com
wine@wichitafallsvineyardsandwinery.com

Tastings, tours: Wed.-Sat. 11 a.m.-5 p.m., Sun.-Tue. by appointment.
Varieties: Cabernet Sauvignon, Merlot, Petite Sirah, Muscato, Riesling, Viognier, Zinfandel dessert and fortified wines, blends and a Sangiovese rosé.

Alton and Lana Gates opened their winery in 2003. Just west of Wichita Falls, it is set in the river bottoms amid 300 native pecan trees near the junction of the Wichita River and Buffalo Creek, not far from Horseshoe Lake.

Wines are aged in oak casks, American and French, while Hungarian oak barrels are used for port-style fortified wine. The Gateses use their wines to make dessert sauces and candles, which they sell in the winery's gift shop.

Worth stopping for: Nearby Wichita Falls' **Hotter 'N Hell Hundred** bicycle event is held at the blistering height of summer every August (www.hh100.org). **Archer City** (www.archercitytx.com) boasts **Booked Up**, the sprawling used and antiquarian bookstore spread over several downtown buildings and operated by Pulitzer-winning novelist and native son Larry McMurtry ("Lonesome Dove"). The **Royal Theater**, the basis for McMurtry's book "The Last Picture Show," which became an Oscar-winning movie, has been restored.

Northeast Texas

At first glance, humid Northeast Texas would seem an unlikely place to grow grapes and make wine.

On the other hand, viticulture has some deep roots — and rootstocks — in this part of the state. Denison, on the Red River up in the far northerly section, was the home of famed horticulturist Thomas Munson. Munson developed many new grape varieties specifically for the climate and soils of the southern and southwestern United States, but he is best known for saving the European wine industry from a looming phylloxera epidemic in the late 19th century with his solution of grafting vinifera vines onto phylloxera-resistant Texas rootstocks. In gratitude, the French city of Cognac recognized Denison as its sister city, and the relationship continues today.

Munson's part of the country is also home to the Homestead Winery, a pioneer in the region; as you drive south from the Red River Valley, the northern plains give way to forests of pine and hardwood, dotted with dogwoods. Threaded with rivers and lakes, Northeast Texas calls itself "The Texas Lake Country."

East Texas has long been known for its berry farms, fruit orchards and vegetable production. Native grapes were among those crops, and anyone who drives the Piney Woods Wine Trail will encounter a lot of wines made from muscadine, mustang and scuppernong grapes, as well as all kinds of berries and other fruits. Many Texans who remember annual family outings to East Texas' pick-your-own berry farms as children may now be making the same drives, but stopping for wine.

The Blue Armadillo Winery

About an hour northeast of Dallas: Take Interstate 30 east to Texas 34 north; in downtown Greenville, turn left on Lee Street (Texas 302). The winery is at the corner of Lee and St. John streets.

Greenville winery: 2702 Lee St., Greenville
903-455-WINE (9463) • www.bluearmadillowinery.com
Tastings, tours: Wed.-Thu. 4-9 p.m., Fri. 4-10 p.m., Sat. 1-10 p.m.

Princeton tasting room: 322 Main St., Princeton
972-736-6377

Hours: Mon.-Sat. noon-midnight, Sun. 10:15 a.m.-4 p.m.
Varieties: Chardonnay, Chenin Blanc, Malbec, Merlot, Pinot Noir, Riesling, blends, port-style fortified wine and sherry.

Opened in 2008 as Greenville's first winery, this cozy winery and tasting room is housed in a century-old building just a block from the Hunt County Courthouse. Aside from its own white and red blends, Blue Armadillo sells bottles from other Texas vintners, including Homestead and Wales Manor. Visitors can also buy cheese trays and flights of wine to drink at the winery, and there's occasional live music.

It's co-owned by ex-DJ Friendlee Buffington and Joe Anselmo, formerly of Carmela Winery in Prosper, who crafts the wines. They've now opened a Blue Armadillo tasting room and bar with a stage for live music in Princeton.

Worth stopping for: The **Audie Murphy/American Cotton Museum**, at 600 Interstate 30 East in Greenville, combines exhibits on the region's cotton-industry heritage and on World War II hero and actor Murphy, who lived in Hunt County. The story of another native son, Chicago White Sox pitcher Monty Stratton, also is told (www.cottonmuseum.com).

The Blue Rooster Winery

About an hour east of Dallas on U.S. 80, or take Interstate 20 east to FM 859 north.

606 W. Pine St. (U.S. 80), Edgewood
903-896-4588 • bluerooster@sbcglobal.net

Tastings, tours: Call for hours.
Varieties: Blends.

Opened in December 2008, the Blue Rooster offers its wines and other Texas bottles, along with salads and sandwiches, at its white cottage tasting room. The food can be taken outdoors to be enjoyed under tall shade trees, and the building is available for private parties.

Worth stopping for: **Edgewood Heritage Park Museum**, in the downtown district, is a nonprofit outdoor architectural museum showcasing 21 restored circa-1900 buildings representing rural life in Texas. It hosts an annual festival in the fall (www.edgewoodheritagefestival.com).

Crump Valley Vineyards

About 4 miles south of Sulphur Springs off Texas 19.

127 Crump Lane, Sulphur Springs
903-975-2327 or 903-975-0468
www.facebook.com/CrumpValleyVineyards
crumpvalley@yahoo.com

Off-site tasting room: Ladies to Linens, 2612 Main St., Winnsboro
Tastings, tours: Hours vary; call or see Facebook page
Varieties: Cabernet Sauvignon, Chardonnay, Merlot, blends.

This young venture south of Sulphur Springs has an off-site vineyard growing Blanc du Bois and Cayuga grapes and a recently planted Blanc du Bois vineyard at the winery.

Partners Travis Crump and Susan Jones haven't been offering regular winery tours, but they operate a tasting room in Winnsboro, about 30 miles to the southeast. Call the winery or check the Facebook page to see when they might be open for visitors.

Fairhaven Vineyards

About 30 miles north of Tyler off U.S. 80.

5340 S. FM 2869, Hawkins • 903-769-4616
www.fairhavenvineyards.com

Tastings, tours: Tue.-Thu. 10 a.m.-6 p.m., Fri. Sat. 10 a.m.-10 p.m.; call for seasonal hours.
Varieties: Baco Noir, Cabernet Sauvignon, Chambourcin, Chardonnay, Black Spanish (Lenoir), Lomanto, Merlot, Norton, Seyval Blanc, Syrah.

In the forested highlands above the Sabine Valley, Fairhaven will sell you not only its estate-bottled and -grown wines but also its vines — and will send crews to lay out and plant your own vineyard.

In its own vineyards, the goal is to produce heat- and drought-tolerant, disease-resistant grape varieties in what it has dubbed the "Heritage Series" of wine grapes; the website calls Fairhaven's breeding vineyard "a living history of American hybrids."

The winery sponsors musical events and is available for special occasions, providing catering and floral arrangements. Other events include classes covering wine history and food pairing, banquets and wine-and-movie nights.

During regular business hours, visitors can enjoy Fairhaven's wine with imported cheeses and cured meats and browse its cellar shop for gifts.

Worth stopping for: The **Old Sabine Bottom Wildlife Management Area** (near Lindale), more than 5,000 acres of bottomland hardwood habitat adjacent to the **Little Sandy National Wildlife Refuge**, offers hiking, wildlife viewing, hunting and fishing (903-881-8233). **Tyler Municipal Rose Garden** comprises 14 acres planted with 400 varieties of roses and many other flora; in October, the garden is the center of the annual Texas Rose Festival (903-531-1212).
Overnighting: Near the rose garden is the **Chilton Grand B&B**, a handsome Greek Revival mansion (903-595-3270, www.chiltongrand.com).

Homestead Winery

Ivanhoe and Denison; tasting room in Grapevine.

www.homesteadwinery.com • info@homesteadwinery.com

Homestead Vineyard & Winery at Ivanhoe: About 85 miles northeast of Dallas; from Bonham, north on Texas 78, northeast on CR 273.

County Road 273, P.O. Box 35, Ivanhoe • 903-583-4281

Tastings, tours: Thu. 1-6 p.m., Fri. 1-9 p.m., Sat. 11 a.m.-7 p.m., Sun. 1-6 p.m.; tours by appointment.

Homestead Winery at Denison: About an hour northeast of Dallas in downtown Denison.

220 W. Main St., Denison • 903-464-0030

Tastings: Mon. 11 a.m.-3 p.m., Tues.-Sat. 11 a.m.-9 p.m.

Homestead Winery at Grapevine tasting room: Downtown Grapevine (North Central Texas region).

211 E. Worth, Grapevine • 817-251-9463

Tastings: Mon.-Wed. 11 a.m.-5:30 p.m., Thu.-Sat. 11 a.m.-9:30 p.m., Sun. noon-5:30 p.m.
Varieties: Cabernet Sauvignon, Chardonnay, Merlot, Syrah, Zinfandel, sparkling wine, port-style fortified wine, sherry, holiday spiced wine.

Barb and Gabe Parker planted their vineyard on a former wheat farm near the little town of Ivanhoe in 1983 and began producing wine in 1989. The owners' forebears have farmed in the region for more than a century.

At their original winery, where they have their main production facility,

Northeast Texas

the Parkers have opened a new Parker House Tasting Room in the restored Parker family farmhouse. And they've expanded their operations to include a production facility and tasting room in Denison and a tasting room in Grapevine.

The Grapevine tasting room, in a Victorian house just off historic Main Street, also displays and sells works of local artists. The Denison tasting room is similarly situated in that city's historic downtown, in a 1920s art-deco building with an art gallery and Italian restaurant; the production facility and cellar are housed in the old Star theater.

Worth stopping for: Denison's **Eisenhower Birthplace State Historic Site** celebrates President Dwight D. Eisenhower, its native son (903-465-8908). Northwest of Denison, **Lake Texoma** offers 650 miles of shoreline adjoining **Eisenhower State Park** (www.tpwd.state.tx.us/spdest/findadest/parks/eisenhower/).

Kiepersol Estates Vineyards & Winery

11 miles south of Tyler off FM 344 E.

www.kiepersol.com • winery@kipersol.com

Winery: 4120 FM 344 E., Tyler • 903-894-8995
Restaurant and B&B: 4120 FM 344 E., Tyler • 903-894-3300
KE Cellars tasting room: 4574 S. Broadway, Tyler • 903-939-9805
KE Bushman's Winery & Celebration Center: 1565 FM 2493 E., Bullard • 903-894-7505

Tastings, tours: Winery Sat. 11 a.m.-sunset; fee for tours. KE Cellars tasting room Mon.-Sat. 11 a.m.-9 p.m. KE Bushman's tasting room Mon.-Fri. 11 a.m.-6 p.m.
Restaurant hours: Tue.-Fri. 5-10 p.m. (last seating at 9), Sat. open all day.
Varieties: Cabernet Sauvignon, Mengsel, Merlot, Moscato, Syrah, Viognier, Zinfandel, sugar-free sweet wines, blends and port-style fortified wine.

In a gated community south of Tyler are vineyards that were put down by a transplanted South African family in 1998 and 1999.

Winemaker and estate manager Marnelle de Wet Durrett, who came to Kiepersol from Napa Valley, ages the estate-grown wines in French and American oak barrels.

The Kiepersol compound boasts not only an upscale restaurant and bed-and-breakfast inn, but also an RV park and a chapel — a quaint brick edifice that can be reserved for small weddings and christenings. The restaurant features prime beef, fresh seafood and a wine list with 150 bottles. There are cooking classes, too, not to mention frequent musical events.

The Kiepersol empire also includes KE Bushman's Winery & Celebration Center, a big special-events and concert venue 10 miles south of Tyler.

Fort Worth Star-Telegram wine critic Jeff Siegel wrote in 2007: "Kiepersol makes award-winning wines with grapes grown in humid East Texas, about as unlikely a place to grow high-quality wine grapes as there is in the state."

Worth stopping for: Tyler Municipal Rose Garden comprises 14 acres planted with 400 varieties of roses and many other flora.

Overnighting: Kiepersol has rooms for overnighting; in Tyler, near the rose garden is the **Chilton Grand B&B**, a handsome Greek Revival mansion (903-595 3270, www.chiltongrand.com).

Los Pinos Ranch Vineyards

4 miles south of Pittsburg, 2 miles west of U.S. 271.

658 County Road 1334, Pittsburg • 903-855-1769
www.lospinosranchvineyards.com
info@LosPinosRanchVineyards.com

Tastings, tours: Fri.-Sat. noon-11 p.m., Sun. noon-6 p.m.; tours on the hour Fri.-Sat. starting at noon. Fee.
Varieties: Black Spanish (Lenoir), Blanc du Bois, Cabernet Sauvignon, Chardonnay, Cynthiana, Muscat Canelli, Sangiovese, Syrah, Vermentino, blends.

Five miles south of Pittsburg amid the lush greenery of East Texas' Camp County, this winery and vineyard were established by a couple transplanted from California. They found immediate acceptance — their 2002 Blanc du Bois sold out in five weeks.

Their wines are made not only from the estate's grapes — Cynthiana, Black Spanish and Blanc du Bois — but from grapes grown in the family's vineyards in West Texas' High Plains region.

Aside from the colorful tasting room, there is a big dining room with jazz Friday and Saturday evenings. The on-site restaurant offers an eclectic menu ranging from panini to nightly entrée specials — tapas are available anytime the winery is open; dinner is served 5-10 p.m. Friday and Saturday.

" We believe wine should not be a pretentious endeavor," says winemaker Jeff Sneed. "So we just make wines that taste good."

Worth stopping for: Pittsburg landmarks include chicken magnate Bo Pilgrim's 75-foot **Prayer Tower at Witness Park**; the mammoth **Bo Pilgrim head**, in front of the Pilgrim's Pride chicken processing plant on U.S. 271 North, the main road into town; Pilgrim's oversized home, known locally as "Cluckingham Palace" for its unrestrained ostentation; and such beloved restaurants as **Hot Links** and **Warrick's**. Also in Pittsburg, an annex to the **Northeast Texas Rural Heritage Depot and Museum** (903-856-1200, www.pittsburgtxmuseum.com) houses a full-sized replica of the fantastical 1902 Ezekiel Airship, built by a Baptist minister who based its design on lines from scripture. Locals insist the airship flew before the Wright Brothers hit Kitty Hawk. North of Pittsburg is the town of Mount Pleasant, home of the popular **Sweet Shop USA**, a chocolate outlet store at 1316 Industrial Road (903 575 0033, www.sweetshopusa.com).

Overnighting: Los Pinos offers two cabins on its wooded winery property, the **Tuscan Cottage** for two and the **Vintner's Cabin** for up to six (903-855-1769). **Carson House Inn and Grille** (Pittsburg) is a B&B and restaurant housed in a Victorian Gothic mansion with a hot tub, a fish pond and more rooms at the back of the property in a vintage railroad car (903-856-2468, www.carsonhouse.com).

Maydelle Country Wines

2 miles east of Maydelle off Texas 84.

175 County Road 2108, Route 4, Box 19102, Rusk
903-795-3915
www.maydellewines.com • steven@maydellewines.com

Tastings, tours: Mon.-Sat. 10 a.m.-6 p.m.
Varieties: Merlot, white Zinfandel; blends and fruit wines including apricot-pear, blackberry, elderberry, grapefruit, lemonade, lime, peach, pear; apple mead. Peach mulled wine available Thanksgiving through Valentine's Day.

Winemaker and pure-East-Texas raconteur Steven Harper transformed a century-old train depot into his tasting room — retrofitting it for toilets, electric lights and air-conditioning — and opened for business in 2004. Nearby, the Texas State Railroad's steam engine still puffs by and rattles the depot for old time's sake.

At this fun family stop, root beer is on tap for children. Aside from wines made from East Texas grapes and other fruits, Maydelle sells wine-related gift items as well as home-brewing and winemaking supplies. All that comes in handy in dry Cherokee County (state law allows wineries and their tasting rooms to operate in dry precincts).

Worth stopping for: The Texas State Railroad, built by prison labor more than a century ago, travels through the piney woods between Rusk and Palestine. Its restored steam engines and passenger cars have been featured in such films as "The Long Riders," "The Great Debaters" and "O Brother, Where Art Thou?" (903-683-2561 or 888-987-2461, www.texasstaterr.com). **Old Farmhouse Pottery**, 232 County Road 1805, Rusk, features works by the singing potter (and writer) David Hendley (903-795-3779, www.farmpots.com).

Paris Vineyards

Eight miles northeast of Paris, about 10 miles south of the Oklahoma border. From Paris, head north on FM 195, turn right onto FM 196, then take the first road on the right, CR 43500.

545 County Road 43500, Paris • 903-785-9463, 903-784-6439
www.parisvineyards.com • winery@parisvineyards.com

Tastings, tours: By appointment and during special events.
Varieties: Blanc du Bois, Chardonnay, Gewürztraminer, Muscat Canelli, Riesling, blends.

Off-site tasting room and wine shop: Paris Vineyards Winery on the Square, 2 Clarksville St., Paris.

Tastings: Mon.-Sat. 1 p.m.-6 p.m. (changes seasonally).

Paris' vineyards are planted on 50 acres of loamy soil flanked by pasture-land and clusters of oaks in the heart of the Red River Valley. The family-run operation is Lamar Country's first commercial winery; its stated mission is to "capture the distinctive characteristics of the Texas terroir," with emphasis on sweet wines.

Though the winery itself is not open to visitors except by appointment, it does host occasional special events, especially for members of its wine club. It's also a member of the Munson Wine Trail.

And the winery has an off-site tasting room and wine shop, Paris Vineyards Winery on the Square, in Paris.

Worth stopping for: Paris' most recognized symbol is, of course, its **Eiffel Tower**. It's 65 feet tall and topped with a bright-red cowboy hat, at the corner of Jefferson Road and Collegiate Drive next to Love Civic Center. *Texas Monthly* deemed downtown Paris' **Culbertson Fountain Plaza** "the prettiest plaza in the state of Texas."

Red Caboose Winery

Meridian is about 60 miles southwest of Fort Worth, between Hico and Hillsboro. From Fort Worth, go south on I-35W to Burleson, turn right on Texas 174 and go south through Cleburne to Meridian. Turn left on FM 2840 and go to CR 1110; turn right and proceed 1.2 miles; the winery is nearly a mile from the green gate on the right.

1147 County Road 1110, Meridian • 254-435-9911
www.redcaboosewinery.com • gary@redcaboosewinery.com
Tastings, tours: Fri.-Sat. 10 a.m.-5 p.m.; may vary seasonally. Tasting fee.

Clifton tasting room: South of Meridian on Texas 6 (Avenue G).
903 S. Ave. G, Clifton • 254-675-0099

Tastings: Thu.-Sat. 10 a.m.-7 p.m., Sun. noon-6 p.m.; may vary seasonally. Tasting fee.

Varieties: Blanc du Bois, Cabernet Franc, Cabernet Sauvignon, Lenoir (Black Spanish), Malbec, Merlot, Syrah, Tempranillo, Viognier, port-style fortified wine and blends.

On the G Lazy M Ranch in Bosque County, just northeast of Meridian, this vineyard and winery produced its first vintage in 2006 and soon picked up medals for its Viognier and a Syrah-Merlot blend.

And Red Caboose is *green*. The winery building, designed by the owner, Dallas architect Gary McKibben, is one of the first wineries in the country to meet the green building criteria of the Leadership in Energy and Environmental Design (LEED). It uses geothermal cooling and chilling, collects rainwater for irrigation and produces its own electricity. A 500-barrel partially subterranean cellar, also geothermically cooled, includes a banquet room.

At the original winery, Red Caboose's new stone patio features a wood-burning outdoor oven, grill and smoker. On the last Friday of each month, it hosts a bring-your-own-picnic "Cork & Fork" party with live music.

Meanwhile, south of Meridian in the town of Clifton, the McKibbens have opened a second Red Caboose tasting room hosting events. Red Caboose is on the Way Out Wineries trail.

Worth stopping for: Meridian State Park boasts a 72-acre lake with fishing, swimming, no-wake boating, an encircling hiking trail and bird-watching. The nearby town of **Hico** (www.hico-tx.com) makes much of a local legend that one of its residents, who lived into the 1950s, was actually Billy the Kid. It has remade its old shopping district into a kind of Wild West miniature Fredericksburg, with antique shops and quirky boutiques. Worth stopping for those with sweet tooths are the

Koffee Kup, famous for its extravagantly meringued pies, and, right next door, **Wiseman House Chocolates**.

Red Road Vineyard and Winery

About 40 minutes southwest of Texarkana. From Mount Pleasant, go 18 miles east on Texas 67, turn right on Martin and left on South Front.

105 S. Front St., Naples • 903-897-9353
www.redroadvineyard.com • rrvw105w@yahoo.com

Tastings, tours: Tue. Thu. 4-8 p.m., Fri. Sat. noon-10 p.m., Sun. noon-6 p.m.; may vary with season.
Varieties: Cabernet Sauvignon, Muscat Canelli, Zinfandel and white Zinfandel, port-style fortified wine, blends.

This family-owned establishment on the Piney Woods Wine Trail is housed in a converted 1890 ice house and power plant. The ice storage area is now the tasting room, with a new deck added. The old meat lockers are used to store grapes and to age wine.

Savannah Winery & Bistro

An hour east of Dallas: From Interstate 20, take exit 523 to Texas 64 east.

574 E. Dallas Highway (Texas 64), Canton
903-567-6810 or 903-714-4097
www.savannahwinerytx.com • savannahwinerytx@aol.com

Tasting hours: Daily 10 a.m.-10 p.m.
Food service: Tues.-Sat. 10 a.m.-10 p.m.
Varieties: Blackberry, blueberry, elderberry/blueberry, plum, peach.

From a little blue-trimmed white cottage right in the thick of Canton's "First Monday Trade Days" — the massive monthly flea market that put this East Texas city on the map — Ed and Flo Pickett serve their own fruit wine along with wines from other regional makers.

The bistro offers appetizers, salads and sandwiches, as well as entrees at dinner. There's live music Thursday, Friday and Saturday nights.

Worth stopping for: Canton First Monday, the sprawling, famous flea market, is touted as among the world's largest. It's held monthly on the four days before the first Monday of the month. For a schedule, see www.firstmondaycanton.com.

St. Rose Vineyard and Winery

Formerly Guerra Vineyard and Winery
Just northeast of Pittsburg, 2 miles east of U.S. 271.

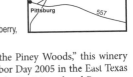

2170 County Road 4110, Pittsburg
903-856-2067 • www.strosewinery.com
St.RoseWinery@gmail.com

Tastings, tours: Sat. noon-5 p.m.
Varieties: Red, white and blush muscadine, apple, cranberry, blueberry, plum, peach, strawberry.

Billing itself as the "Muscadine Winery of the Piney Woods," this winery opened as Guerra Vineyard and Winery on Labor Day 2005 in the East Texas town of Pittsburg. It started as a family venture by Dr. Manuel and Rosemary Guerra, who were joined by their son-in-law and daughter, Mark and Ann Arras.

The winery specializes in wines made from muscadine grapes, both dry and dessert varieties, as well as fruit wines. Rosemary Guerra planted her first muscadine grapes in 1994, and it was in her memory that the Arras renamed the winery St. Rose.

The tasting room, where winemaking kits and muscadine juice are sold alone with the St. Rose wines, is in a converted century-old sweet-potato smokehouse. Outside in a pine-tree setting are picnic tables, a 20-acre pond, muscadine vineyards and fruit orchards.

Worth stopping for: See **Los Pinos Ranch Vineyards** listing, page 96.

Sweet Dreams Winery

From Palestine, go north on Brushy Creek Road (FM 315) for 10 miles; turn right (east) on CR 444, then right (south) on CR 441; winery is another quarter-mile on the left.

2549 Anderson County Road 441, Palestine
903-549-2027 • www.sweetdreamswinery.com
sweetdreamswinery@yahoo.com

Tastings, tours: Sat. 11 a.m.-8 p.m.; may vary seasonally; call for weekday appointments. Tasting fee.
Varieties: Wines made from muscadine, Concord and wild mustang grapes; fruit wines including blackberry-grape, blueberry, honey-pear, honey-raspberry, jalapeño, muscadine, peach-blackberry, pear, plum rosé, strawberry.

Firefighter Mike Pell, whose bad knees kept him up nights, found he slept much better after a glass of the homemade wine he'd bought at an auction. When his supply ran out, Pell and his schoolteacher wife Sandra, who were also partners in a Christmas tree farm, decided to make their own, using blackberries from their property.

Before the Pells got the winemaking bug, the *Palestine Herald Press* noted, this area of East Texas was far better known for moonshine stills than for wines. Now the Pells make a variety of fruit wines.

Outside, there's a covered porch and patio, and family and friends still pitch in to pick and prepare fruit, label bottles and wait on customers.

Worth stopping for: See **Maydelle Country Wines** listing, page 97.

Tara Vineyard & Winery

Northwest of Athens. From Dallas, head southeast on Texas 175; after Eustace, go 6.5 miles and turn left on CR 3918, then left on CR 3914, then go one mile.

8603 County Road 3914, Athens • 903-675-7023
www.tarawinery.com • slpoftexas@tarawinery.com

Tastings tours: Sun., Tue.-Wed. 11:30 a.m.-sunset, Thu.-Sat. 11:30 a.m.-11 p.m., other times by appointment. Tours at 2:30 p.m. Sat. and by reservation. Fee.
Varieties: Barbera, Blanc du Bois, Cabernet Franc, Chardonnay, Cynthiana (Norton), Black Spanish (Lenoir) blush, Merlot, Petite Sirah, Syrah, Zinfandel, Cabernet Sauvignon, Madeira, blends.

Don't be surprised if Henderson County's first winery evokes a bit of the antebellum South: The name is borrowed from the plantation in *Gone With the Wind*. To reinforce the impression, a 19th-century mansion, formerly the Murchison home, now serves as a stately bed-and-breakfast inn.

Tara produces Blanc du Bois wine from its own vineyard and a variety of wines both dry and sweet from Texas-grown grapes as well as other American grapes. The estate's flagstone patio hosts occasional live music, and on Saturday nights the inn hosts a reservations-only piano bar.

The winery operates a gourmet restaurant, Cellar Door, on the grounds, serving lunch and dinner Thursday through Sunday; call ahead for reservations. There's live jazz Thursday nights.

Texas Roads Winery

1 block west of the courthouse in downtown Canton.

134 W. Dallas St., Canton • 903-567-6801
www.texasroadswinery.com • texasroadswinery@yahoo.com

Tastings, tours: Wed.-Sat. 3-11 p.m.; on First Monday Trade Days weekends, open at 1 p.m. Sat. and 1-7 p.m. Sun.; open 1-7 p.m. third Sundays for music.
Varieties: Gewürztraminer, Merlot, Syrah, Zinfandel, blends.

This storefront winery, which makes three sweet wines and sells wines from other Texas wineries, affects a '50s Harley-Davidson theme.

Texas Roads functions as a nightlife venue for Canton, with karaoke Wednesdays and Thursdays, live rock Fridays and Saturdays and an acoustic jam session from 3 to 7 p.m. every third Sunday of the month.

Worth stopping for: See **Savannah Winery & Bistro** listing, page 100.

Texas Vineyard & Smokehaus

About 5 miles south of Palestine, east of U.S. 79/84. From Dallas, take Interstate 45 to exit 198 at Fairfield, go east on U.S. 84, east on U.S. 79, right on Texas 294, left on FM 1990, left on CR 2133.

2442 Anderson County Road 2133, Palestine • 903-538-2950
www.texasvineyard.org • texasvineyard@embarqmail.com

Tastings, tours: Wed.-Sun. noon-7 p.m.; may change with season; tours and tastings free.
Varieties: Cabernet Sauvignon, Merlot, Muscat, Riesling, Syrah, Zinfandel, muscadine, port-style fortified wine and sweet muscadine fortified wine, sparkling wine, blends.

This family-run winery and bistro offers its own smoked turkeys and hams along with an ambitious selection of varietal wines and blends.

The wines are all made, the winery promises, from Texas-grown grapes, and served, along with appetizers and pizzas, in the tasting room or on the winery's balcony overlooking a pond. Catering, event hosting and gift baskets are also offered, along with occasional live music.

Worth stopping for: See **Maydelle Country Wines** listing, page 97.

Southeast Texas

It's a tribute to the orneriness some consider to be a part of Texans' collective DNA that there should be wineries in this hot and humid part of Texas. Southeast Texas, after all, is most inimical to the growing of grapes, at least the kind of grapes that the typical bottle of wine is made from.

But wineries there are — 16 at last count, not counting several tasting rooms such as Braman in Refugio and Richmond, selling wines made out of state. And all in country that ranges from rolling prairie to deep piney woods to coastal flatlands. Several wineries are clustered northwest of Houston, with a few more south of that vast city.

But the mover and shaker in the region is also the oldest, the largest and the farthest north — the juggernaut that is Messina Hof, near Bryan, a veritable Disneyland of a winery whose owners have been active from the first in state wine circles.

The typical wine grapes known as vinifera struggle under most of this region's conditions, so growers often plant native New World varieties such as Black Spanish, Blanc du Bois and Norton; winemakers like Raymond Haak of Haak Vineyards near Galveston have had notable success with them. You'll also see wine made from muscadine grapes, fruit, hibiscus flowers and honey — even jalapeños and prickly pear fruits.

Bernhardt Winery

Between Conroe and Navasota off Texas 105, a little more than an hour northwest of Houston. From Houston, north on Texas 249, north on FM 1488/Magnolia Parkway, left on FM 1774, right on Texas 105, left on CR 204, winery on the left. Or take I-45 to Conroe, go west on Texas 105 for 24 miles and turn right on CR 204.

9043 County Road 204, Plantersville
936-894-9829 or 936-520-8684
www.bernhardtwinery.com • jerry@bernhardtwinery.com

Tastings, tours: Tue.-Fri. noon-5 p.m., Sat. noon-6 p.m., Sun. 1-5 p.m.; by appointment other times. Fee.
Varieties: Cabernet Sauvignon, Chardonnay, Merlot, Pinot Grigio, red and white blends, muscadine, port-style fortified wine.

This family-run venture produces about 6,000 gallons of wine annually while trying to provide a fun experience for visitors.

You can sip Bernhardt's wines during lawn concerts at sunset each Sunday from mid-April though mid-November (check the website for the On-the-Porch Sunset Concert Series), or picnic in the winery's pecan grove and enjoy a panoramic view.

The hilltop Tuscan-style tasting room overlooks verdant hills. Aside from wines, it sells wine-related gifts, jellies, jams and sauces.

The grounds also boast a bed-and-breakfast called the Loft over the tasting room. A stay includes a complimentary bottle of wine, hors d'oeuvre and a glass of wine at sunset, followed the next morning with a continental-style breakfast in your room or on the patio.

The events room can be contracted for receptions and other occasions, and the winery participates in events on the Bluebonnet Wine Trail.

Worth stopping for: Montgomery, 9 miles to the west, is the birthplace of the Texas flag and home to numerous antique shops. **Navasota**, just 7 miles from the winery and famous for its honeybee breeding, also has a number of antique shops.

Bruno & George Winery

In Sour Lake, 18 miles west of Beaumont.

From Beaumont: Take Texas 105 to Sour Lake; at red light, turn left on Texas 326, then left on Old Beaumont Road before the elementary school; turn right on Nevada Street, then right on Messina Road to the winery.

From Houston: Take U.S. 90 E to Nome; turn left on Texas 326 and continue north to Sour Lake, then right on Old Beaumont Road, right on Nevada Street, right on Messina Road to the winery.

400 Messina Road, Sour Lake • 409-287-1212 or 409-963-8235
www.brunoandgeorge.com • shawn@brunoandgeorge.com or misha@brunoandgeorge.com

Tastings, tours: By appointment.
Varieties: Raisin, blueberry, cranberry, pear, strawberry, raisin, raspberry.

This small establishment is resurrecting the old art of making raisin wine, illegal in Texas until a 1999 law removed dried fruit from a list of banned ingredients for commercial wine. This was a triumph for founder Shawn Bruno, who had lobbied for the change so he could make commercial use of the old Sicilian family recipe brought over by his grandfather.

He and his wife Misha also make fruit wine along with their award-winning, port-like "Other Than Standard" raisin wine.

The winery and a new pavilion are available for weddings and events.

Worth stopping for: **Big Thicket National Preserve**, a 100,000-acre-plus arc stretching north and west from Beaumont with a visitor center just north of Kountze, offers hiking, camping, biking, horseback riding, canoeing and kayaking, bird-watching, nature walks, hunting, trapping and fishing. It was designated a UNESCO Biosphere Reserve in 1981 and a Globally Important Bird Area in 2001 (409-951-6700; www.nps.gov/bith). **Spindletop Gladys City Boomtown Museum** (Beaumont) brings back the city's oil-boom past with a re-creation of an early oil-strike boomtown (409-835-0823, www.spindletop.org).

Overnighting: **Ethridge Farm B&B** (Kountze) offers a rustic lodge and cabins in a restful setting (409-898-2710 or 409-246-3978, www.ethridgefarm.com).

Pelt Farm B&B (Kountze) is an 1840 log dogtrot cabin on a farm with antique roses, butterflies, large oaks, longhorn cattle, Choctaw horses and yellow blackmouth cur dogs (409-287-3300, www.peltfarm.com).

Circle S Vineyards

In the southwest Houston suburb of Sugar Land. From Houston, drive south on U.S. 59 to Sugar Land; take the Dairy Ashford/Sugar Creek exit north to the Sugar Point Center on your left.

9920 U.S. 90A, Suite B 268, Sugar Land • 281-265-9463
www.circlesvineyards.com • info@circlesvineyards.com

Tastings, tours: Tue.-Thu. 1-7:30 p.m., Fri.-Sat. 11 a.m.-8:30 p.m., Sun. noon-5 p.m.

Varieties: Barbera, Cabernet Sauvignon and white Cabernet Sauvignon, Chardonnay, Merlot, Montepulciano, Pinot Noir, Sangiovese, Syrah, Tempranillo, Zinfandel, blush and blends; raspberry.

The vineyards are in Centerville (and some of the grapes are sourced from Tuscany), but the winery is in the Houston suburb of Sugar Land, where sculptor Dave Stacy and his wife Helen craft a variety of French, Spanish and Italian varietals as well as novelties such as blackberry port-style fortified wine and jalapeño wine.

Their suburban winery offers tastings in a living-room setting stocked with books and board games and schedules wine classes and dinners. Reception rooms are available for special occasions.

Fourth-generation winemakers, the Stacys donate 5 percent of corporate proceeds to charities and religious groups.

Worth stopping for: **George Ranch Historical Park** in nearby Richmond offers a glimpse of a historic four-generation ranch (281-343-0218; www.georgeranch.org).

Colony Cellars

About 30 miles northwest of Houston. From Houston, take I-10 to Texas 359 north to Monaville; turn right at the blinking yellow light on Richard Frey Road and follow the road about 2 miles to the winery on the right.

35955 Richard Frey Road, Waller • 979-826-3995
www.colonycellars.com • info@colonycellars.com

Tastings, tours: Thu.-Sun. 10 a.m.-6 p.m.; tastings free. Miniature trolley tours daily at 11 a.m., 1 and 3 p.m. by reservation only (fee).
Varieties: Red, blush and white blends.

On 50 acres of rolling prairie with three ponds and stands of evergreens, the vineyard produces seven grape varieties that go into Colony's red, blush and white blends. The winery's tasting room and gift shop has a pond-side patio, and the grounds offer picnic sites complete with ducks, goats and one of the state's largest Japanese carp (koi) ponds.

The winery also boasts a 1.5-mile vineyard train ride, a bamboo jungle maze, an aviary that gives away a parakeet with the purchase of a birdcage and an observation deck with a contraption called a "living machine." In winter, visitors can cut their own Christmas trees at the evergreen farm.

The whole enterprise is the dream of Don Corley, a former banker and university computer-science department chairman, who employs a French winemaking technique known as whole-cluster fermentation. The grapes start fermenting in airless storage, all berries and stems intact, before they are crushed. The aim is to get a fresher berry aroma.

"We didn't need just another winery," Corley says. "We wanted to do something different, and that's what we got." Moreover, Corley takes pride in using screw tops, which he stoutly maintains are superior to cork.

Colony's facilities are available for family or business gatherings. And call for a variety of events: There's Thirsty Thursday, with a special discount on cases, followed by Fondue Friday, featuring various fondues paired with wine, and Slider Saturdays, offering wine and baby burgers.

Worth stopping for: Liendo Plantation, northwest of Waller near Hempstead, was one of Texas' earliest and most celebrated cotton plantations. Gen. George Armstrong Custer was billeted there after the Civil War, and it was later occupied by sculptor Elisabet Ney. It's open the first Saturday of most months and hosts Civil War Weekend, a period-dress battle reenactment, annually in mid-November (979-826-3126, www.liendo.org).

Darcy's Vineyard

Between Shiner and Hallettsville.

7952 Farm-to-Market 1891, Hallettsville • 713-306-4236
www.darcysvineyard.com • darcy@darcysvineyard.com

Tastings, tours: Sat. 10 a.m-5 p.m. and by appointment
Varieties: Chardonnay, Sangiovese and blends; mead.

Situated on 24 acres of rolling hills between Hallettsville and the brewing town of Shiner, this winery is Lavaca County's first, having sold its first wine at local market days before opening its tasting room. It makes its wine in very small batches, from 30 to 60 gallons each.

The family began planting vines for the venture in 2005, experimenting with a number of varieties to find the right match for conditions in this corner of Texas. The vineyard consists primarily of red-wine grapes Lomanto and Champanel — hybrids developed by Texas wine-grape legend T.V. Munson — as well as Sangiovese, the principal grape in Chianti.

The family-friendly winery has board games for kids and a shaded sandbox outside, along with grazing longhorns, guinea hens and winery kittens, not to mention fields of bluebonnets during wildflower season and a picnic area with scenic hillside views.

Worth stopping for: Nearby Shiner is the home of Shiner beer — brewed at the historic and celebrated **Spoetzl Brewery** (361-594-4294, www.shiner.com), which offers weekday tours (closed weekends).

Haak Vineyards & Winery

Between Alvin and Galveston, about 2 miles south of Texas 6.

6310 Ave. T, Santa Fe • 409-925-1401
www.haakwine.com • raymond@haak.com

Tastings, tours: Mon.-Fri. 11 a.m.-6 p.m., Sat. 11 a.m.-7 p.m., Sun. noon-5 p.m. (special events may affect hours; call to check). Tours on the hour (fee); call ahead for groups.
Varieties: Blanc du Bois, Cabernet Sauvignon, Gewürztraminer, Sauvignon Blanc, Malbec, Tempranillo, blends, red and white port-style fortified wines and madeiras.

With two grapevines —a 10th-anniversary gift — Raymond and Gladys Haak began as a hobby what would become the first commercial winery in Galveston County. It was unlikely terrain for grape-growing, but the wines crafted by this electrical engineer and accountant have proved their worth

108

at a slew of competitions — especially the semi-sweet, dry and dessert wines they make from Blanc du Bois grapes.

Today they have a 25,000-square-foot winery with a 1,800-square-foot cellar. Now that demand has outpaced their 3-acre vineyard's supply, the Haaks bring in grapes from California and Texas growers.

The couple also has planted an experimental half-acre olive orchard.

Texas Monthly magazine raved: "Haak Winery is not just a place to go sample and buy wines. The 12-acre estate boasts an entertainment pavilion for the many music concerts and on-site weddings. And guests can expect a full summer concert series with gourmet picnic dinners ... Seasonal events fill the calendar all year." Check the website for events.

Worth stopping for: Galveston offers not only long stretches of open beach but streets full of gorgeous old historic houses, lavishly gargoyled and gingerbreaded. **The Strand (Galveston),** lined with boutiques, eateries and gift shops, is the pride of this island city (www.galveston.com). Other attractions include **Elissa,** a refurbished tall ship at the **Texas Seaport Museum** (www. galvestonhistory.org/Texas_Seaport_Museum.asp), and **Moody Gardens'** massive triple pyramids, housing a rain forest display, an aquarium and a science museum, plus theaters, a beach, a bayou paddlewheeler ride, golf course and hotel (409-741-8484 or 800-582-4673, www.moody-gardens.com). Galveston is awash in big, bustling seafood houses, but on the Gulf something a little more laid-back seems appropriate: In oyster season, the ramshackle **Sonny's Place** is a longtime favorite for oyster mugs and oyster buns (1206 19th St., 409-763-9602), or try a fragrant muffuletta sandwich at **Maceo Spice & Import Co.** (2706 Market St., 409-763-3331).

Overnighting: The Wyndham hotel chain runs two of the city's most atmospheric and historic hotels: The century-old **Hotel Galvez & Spa,** spiffed up with a renovation a few years ago, overlooks the Gulf of Mexico from the other side of Seawall Boulevard (409-765-7721, www.wyndham.com/hotels/GLSHG/main.wnt). The **Tremont House** offers Victorian elegance with a rooftop lounge just off the Strand (409-763-0300, www.thetremonthouse.com).

Messina Hof Winery & Resort

7 miles northeast of Bryan off Texas 6.
From Houston: Take U.S. 290 west to Texas 6; go north to Bryan. Exit Old Reliance Road in Bryan, turning right, and follow the signs to the winery.
From Austin: Take U.S. 290 east to Texas 21; go east to Bryan. Exit Texas 6 South; take Old Reliance Road to the left and follow the signs to the winery.

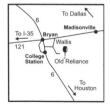

4545 Old Reliance Road, Bryan
979-778-9463 or 800-736-9463
www.messinahof.com • wine@messinahof.com

Tasting room: Mon.-Sat. 10 a.m.-7 p.m.; Sun. 11 a.m.-6 p.m. Fee.

Tours: Mon.-Fri. 1, 2:30 and 5:30 p.m. (sunset tours at 7 p.m. Fri. by reservation); Sat. 11 a.m., 12:30, 2:30, 4 and 5:30 p.m.; Sun. 12:30, 2:30 and 4 p.m. Fee charged; private tours by appointment.
Restaurant: Wed.-Sat. 11 a.m.-4 p.m. and 5-9 p.m., Sun. 11 a.m.-6 p.m.
Wine bar: Mon.-Thu. 11 a.m.-7 p.m., Fri.-Sat. 11 a.m.-9 p.m., Sun. 11 a.m.-6 p.m.
Varieties: Cabernet Franc, Cabernet Sauvignon, Chardonnay, Chenin Blanc, Gewürztraminer, Muscat Canelli, Pinot Grigio, Pinot Noir, Merlot, Riesling, Sauvignon Blanc, Shiraz and blends; port-style fortified wines, sherries, sparkling wine.

Messina Hof Hill Country Tasting Room: 9666 U.S. 290 E., Fredericksburg • 830-990-4653
www.messinahof.com/mhhillcountry.php
Tastings: Sun.-Wed. 11 a.m.-6 p.m., Thu.-Sat. 11 a.m.-7 p.m.

Messina Hof's 100-acre estate includes a 42-acre vineyard, the winery, the Vintage House restaurant, the Winemaster's Wine Bar, a guest center, a gift shop and the Villa at Messina Hof bed and breakfast inn.

Named for the communities in Italy (Messina) and Germany (Hof) that were home to the forebears of owners Paul and Merrill Bonarrigo, this winery was among the first in Texas to turn itself into a tourist destination. Messina Hof has been raking in the medals and media notice since the Bonarrigos planted their first vines in 1977.

It's a tribute to the couple's marketing skills that Messina Hof, situated in a part of Texas not noted for its climate or terroir vis-à-vis grapes, ranks in the top five in sales among Texas wineries. The Bonarrigos have built a veritable wine theme park in Bryan, and now they're exporting the formula to the rest of Texas, starting with their Messina Hof Hill Country tasting room east of Fredericksburg.

The winery's lakeside guest center is in Bryan's restored Howell House, a French-style manor constructed in the early 1900s for the Ursuline Sisters and later the home of a former U.S. ambassador. The rose garden, home to 3,500 white rosebushes, can be rented for weddings and other events.

The Villa B&B is adorned with 27 stained-glass windows made centuries ago in Spain for a church in Donna, Texas. Each antique-filled room pays homage to a romantic figure or couple: Napoleon and Josephine, Romeo and Juliet, Lancelot and Guinevere, Thomas Jefferson — conspicuously without a named paramour.

On Friday evenings, weather permitting, Messina Hof runs a reservations-only 7 p.m. sunset tour through the vineyard, followed by a flight of four wines paired with menu selections from the wine bar.

Worth stopping for: The **George Bush Presidential Library and Museum**, on Texas A&M University's vast campus in College Station, offers insights into the life and presidency of our 41st president, George H.W. Bush (979-691-4000, www.bushlibrary.tamu.edu). **Cafe Eccell** (College Station) is a comfortable off campus eatery with high-quality, eclectic fare (979-846-7908).

Piney Woods Country Winery & Vineyards

Northwest of Orange just off Interstate 10. From Houston or Beaumont: East on Interstate 10; at Orange, take exit 876 and continue east on the frontage road to the next U-turn under the freeway; go left (west) on Lutcher Drive (frontage road), right on Tejas Parkway and right on Willow Drive.

3408 Willow Drive, Orange • 409-883-5408
www.pineywoodswines.com • pineywoods1@gmail.com

Tastings, tours: Mon.-Sat. 9 a.m.-5 p.m., closed Sun.
Varieties: Red, white and blush muscadine; fruit wines including blackberry, blueberry, peach, plum; flavored wines including Sweet Tooth Cherry Chocolates and Texas Pecan Mocca; port-style fortified wines.

Nestled in the woods near Adams Bayou, Piney Woods has specialized in "country wines" since selling its first batch in 1987. Vintner Alfred Flies produces several types of muscadine wine along with fruit and flavored wines.

It all began with a single tree that produced far more plums than Flies' family could consume. He remembered the plum wine his father had made in Oklahoma. His first batch turned out well, and eventually he gave up the interior-design business to devote himself to putting Southeast Texas on the wine map.

Worth stopping for: In Orange, time is frozen at the **Farmer's Mercantile**, a 1920s-era Texas general store (409-883-2941).

Pleasant Hill Winery

From Brenham, go south on Texas 36 and west (right) on Salem Road.

1441 Salem Road, Brenham • 979-830-VINE (8463)
pleasanthillwinery.com • info@pleasanthillwinery.com

Tastings: Sat. 11 a.m.-6 p.m., Sun. noon-5 p.m.
Tours: Sat. hourly from 11:30 a.m. to 4:30 p.m., Sun. hourly from 12:30 to 3:30 p.m. Fee.

Varieties: Blanc du Bois, Cabernet Sauvignon, Sangiovese, Sauvignon Blanc, blends, port-style wines.

Housed in a reconstructed old barn, the winery sits on rolling hills just south of Brenham and features traditional winemaking equipment. On display is an extensive collection of corkscrews and winemaking artifacts.

The Austin Chronicle said: "The cellar looks like a mad scientist's laboratory, with tanks and barrels filling nearly every inch. Upstairs is the tasting room, with its wonderful view of the hills and a small gift shop."

Check the website for catered tastings of new releases, dinner theater performances and Texas Bluebonnet Wine Trail events.

Worth stopping for: Blue Bell Creameries is a popular destination in Brenham for tour groups and sightseeing families. The "little dairy in the country" is not so tiny any more, what with producing ever-greater quantities of ice cream for generations of eager Texans (800-327-8135, www. bluebell.com). Brenham locals in the know eat at downtown's **Funky Art Café**, an affordable, eclectic, fun eatery with an internet coffee bar and gift shop (979-836-5220, www.funkyartcafe. com). The **Antique Rose Emporium** display garden in Independence offers charmingly planted paths, ponds, water gardens, arbors and gazebos, plus antique rose varieties for sale (979-836-5548, www.antiqueroseemporium.com).

Overnighting: At **Brenham's Ant Street Inn**, you can spend the night downtown in a room filled with handsome antiques (800-805-2600 or 800-481-1951). For country accommodations, **Mariposa Ranch Bed & Breakfast**, north of Brenham, offers period rooms in an 1836 Greek Revival home, an 1870 plantation-style mansion and several other buildings on a 100-acre spread (877-647-4774, www.mariposaranch.com).

Retreat Hill Winery & Vineyard

Between Hempstead and Navasota.

15551 Farm-to-Market 362, Navasota • 936-825-8282
www.retreathill.com • RHW-events@RetreatHill.com

Tastings, tours: Sat. 11 a.m.-6 p.m., Sun. noon-5 p.m.
Varieties: Gewürztraminer, Riesling, Syrah, Zinfandel, blends, port-style fortified wine, madeira.

Downtown Montgomery satellite winery and sales room:
Retreat Hill Cellars, 211 Liberty St. (Texas 149), Montgomery • 936-449-5285
Tastings: Wed.-Sat. 11 a.m.-7 p.m., Sun. noon-6 p.m.

This young winery is named for nearby Groce's Retreat, the home of Jared Groce, where George C. Childress took refuge to write Texas' Declaration of

Independence from Mexico.

Owner and winemaker Billy S. Cox Jr. is a self-described renaissance man — he has been an engineer, television host and amateur chef — who dreamed for years of owning a vineyard and winery.

This ambition was realized in 2007 when be acquired 12 acres in Grimes County. Two years later, his winery was open for business, buying grapes from Texas and other grape-growing states while the vines were being established. Its first awards soon followed.

Next, Cox opened Retreat Hill Cellars in Montgomery's old First State Bank, which went bust during the Depression. "We are going to make small batches of wine in the vault and perhaps prepare an intimate table setting for two or four people for a very unique dining experience," he says.

Worth stopping for: Navasota, famous for its honeybee breeding, houses a number of antique shops. At the **Washington-on-the-Brazos State Historic Site** (www.tpwd.state.tx.us/spdest/findadest/parks/washington_on_the_brazos/), where Texas declared its independence from Mexico, are the **Star of the Republic Museum**, **Independence Hall** and **Barrington Living History Farm**, which re-creates mid-1800s farm life at the historic home of the last president of the Republic of Texas, Anson Jones (936-878-2214). Next to the park, on FM 1155 in Washington, is **R Place**, a rescued old grocery store that serves barbecue Friday-Sunday and special dinners Saturday nights; wine too (936-878-1925). Also see **Colony Cellars** listing, page 107.

Rosemary's Vineyard & Winery

Five miles east of La Grange on Texas 71. From Austin, take Texas 71 east through La Grange. From Houston, take I-10 west toward Columbus, taking Exit 71 west toward Austin.

5521 Texas 71 E., La Grange • 979-249-2109
http://wines-made-in-texas.com/default.aspx
rosemarysvineyard1@yahoo.com

Tastings, tours: Thu.-Sun. noon-sunset. Fee.
Varieties: Blanc du Bois, Chardonnay, Lenoir, Merlot, muscadine, port-style fortified wine.

Emmett and Beatrice Schulze planted their first vines in 2000 and then gave up their respective day jobs as a home remodeling contractor and restaurateur to open Fayette County's first winery in 2006.

Visitors can bring picnic lunches to enjoy with the family's wines, and homegrown blackberries are seasonally available.

Worth stopping for: Downtown **La Grange** boasts a number of fine old buildings, including a circa-1890 courthouse and the **Muster Oak**, where Capt. Nicholas Dawson gathered his men before the battle at Salado Creek at San Antonio in 1842.

Saddlehorn Winery

In Washington County between Houston and Austin, on FM 1948 one mile northwest of U.S. 290.

958 Farm-to-Market Road 1948, Burton • 979-289-3858
www.saddlehornwinery.com • info@saddlehornwinery.com

Tastings, tours: Tue.-Sun. 11 a.m.-6 p.m. Fee.
Varieties: Blanc du Bois, Black Spanish (Lenoir), Chardonnay, Merlot, Muscat, port-style and muscadine wine.

On the scenic, rolling hills of a 360-acre ranch halfway between Houston and Austin, Saddlehorn offers a peaceful setting to enjoy estate-grown Blanc du Bois and Black Spanish wines.

The winery and tasting room, which opened in 2010, are housed in a renovated 12,000-square-foot horse barn. Only grapes from Washington County are used; Saddlehorn also grows blackberries for sale in season.

Saddlehorn is on the Texas Bluebonnet Wine Trail.

Worth stopping for/overnighting: See **Pleasant Hill Winery** listing, page 111.

Texas SouthWind Vineyard and Winery

Just north of Refugio on Alt. U.S. 77/U.S. 183.

16375 U.S. 183 S., Refugio • 361-526-4662
www.texassouthwind.com • staggsdrld@wildblue.net

Tastings, tours: Mon.-Sat. 11 a.m.-7 p.m., Sun. by appointment
Varieties: Blanc du Bois, Cabernet Sauvignon, Malbec, Muscat Canelli, Sauvignon Blanc, Tempranillo; peach, blackberry.

Established on a 145-acre ranch in 2009, Texas SouthWind is operated by the Staggs family in an area better known for Santa Gertrudis on the hoof than Gewürztraminer in a glass. Family-owned and faith-based, the winery makes white, red, dessert and fruit wines and puts a Bible verse on each of its bottles. There's live music on the first Saturday of each month.

Worth stopping for: In Refugio is another wine destination, the tasting room of Braman Winery (361-526-2722, www.bramanwine.com). The most famous winter visitors to the **Aransas National Wildlife Refuge** are the endangered whooping cranes, but many other migratory birds, as well as javelinas and alligators, are found there as well. Attractions in the nearby Gulf Coast city of Corpus Christi include the **USS Lexington** aircraft carrier (361-888-4873, www.usslexington.com), the **South Texas Botanical Gardens & Nature Center** (361-852-2100, www.stxbot.org) and the **Texas State Aquarium** (361-881-1200, www.texasstateaquarium.org); nearby is **Padre Island National Seashore** (www.nps.gov/pais/index.htm). **Port Aransas** on Mustang Island, a longtime getaway destination for Texas beach-lovers, is nearby as well (www.portaransas.org).

Texas Star Winery

East of College Station and northwest of Houston.

From College Station, take Texas 30 east, go right on FM 2562, left on FM 149 and continue 5.3 miles. Immediately after the Montgomery County line sign, turn right onto a common driveway; in a half-mile, enter gate with winery's brand on the left.

From the Woodlands/Conroe, take Interstate 45 north, exit west on Texas 105, turn right on FM 149, then follow above directions.

29311 FM 149, Richards • 936-851-2400
www.texasstarwinery.com • info@texasstarwinery.com

Tastings, tours: Fri.-Sat. 1-5 p.m. and by appointment.
Varieties: Hibiscus, prickly pear and a sweet sherry-style wine.

Right on the county line between Montgomery and Grimes counties, this winery is near the Sam Houston National Forest on scenic FM 149, which is also known as Montgomery Trace.

Sometimes good things emerge from bad situations. Earl Love had been an amateur winemaker for years — had even won some prizes in amateur competitions — when he was involuntarily retired in 2008 and decided to pursue his dream to create a different sort of wine. hibiscus flower (sparkling and still) and true-Texas prickly-pear cactus wines.

The winery, on the Texas Bluebonnet Wine Trail, schedules special events such as cooking classes.

Worth stopping for: Sam Houston National Forest, covering more than 260,000 acres in three counties, offers camping and hiking trails, hunting, fishing and boating on lakes Livingston and Conroe (936-569-7981, http://www.tpwd.state.tx.us/huntwild/hunt/wma/find_a_wma/list/?id=30). **Washington-on-the-Brazos State Historic Site** (www.tpwd.state.tx.us/spdest/findadest/parks/

washington_on_the_brazos/), where Texas declared its independence from Mexico, includes the **Star of the Republic Museum, Independence Hall** and **Barrington Living History Farm**, which re-creates mid-1800s farm life at the historic home of the last president of the Republic of Texas, Anson Jones (936-878-2214, www.tpwd.state.tx.us/spdest/findadest/parks/barrington_farm/).

White House Winery

Just southeast of Navasota and an hour northwest of Houston. From Houston, go west on U.S. 290, north on FM 362

15828 Farm-to-Market Road 362, White Hall • 281-702-2850
www.whitehousewinery.net • whitehousewinery@yahoo.com

Tastings, tours: Fri. 3-6 p.m., Sat.-Sun. noon-6 p.m.
Varieties: Cabernet Sauvignon, Chardonnay, Chianti, Riesling, Zinfandel and blends.

Gary Hahne's family worked for Lyndon B. Johnson for several generations, and Hahne is hoping to bring to East Texas some of the hospitality the clan helped mount for the Texas White House at LBJ's ranch in Stonewall.

The winery is designed to resemble that Hill Country edifice, which family members helped redesign and expand in the 1950s, and visitors to the winery can peruse a gallery of photos from that presidential connection.

Years in the making, the White House Winery finally opened its doors in 2011, just up the road from Retreat Hill Winery & Vineyard.

Worth stopping for: See **Retreat Hill Winery & Vineyard**, page 112.

Windy Winery

Between Brenham and Independence off FM 50. From Brenham, go northeast on Texas 105, north (left) on FM 50; turn east (right) on CR 65; follow 65 until it becomes Clover Road (CR 64).

4232 Clover Road, Brenham • 979-836-7010
www.windywinery.com • info@windyhillwinery.net

Tastings, tours: Wed.-Fri. noon-5 p.m.; Sat. 11 a.m.-6 p.m.; Sun. 1-5 p.m.
Varieties: Blanc du Bois, Champanel, Shiraz, Lenoir (Black Spanish), port, blends.

This family-owned winery, deep in Blue Bell Ice Cream country, was opened in 2005. After establishing a six-acre vineyard, August and Linda

Meitzen, both ceramic artists, remodeled a barn with recycled lumber from a century-old farmhouse, then added stained glass. They are adamant about using only grapes grown in Texas, including some from their own vineyard.

Aside from the tasting room, the winery has a gift shop selling the couple's pottery and stained glass.

"Basically, it's stepping back in time. We do everything by hand," the couple says. "The only thing electric is the crusher. Wine is hand-bottled."

Formerly called Windy Hill, the winery offers a scenic view from its hilltop site, especially during bluebonnet season. The winery, on the Texas Bluebonnet Wine Trail, is available for special events.

Worth stopping for/overnighting: See **Pleasant Hill Winery** listing, page 111, and **Retreat Hill Winery and Vineyard** listing, page 112.

Yepez Vineyard

East of Baytown near Trinity Bay. From Interstate 10, take FM 3180 south to FM 2354 just past Fisher Road.

12739 Farm-to-Market Road 2354, Baytown
281-573-4139 or 281-804-3410
www.yepezvineyard.com
yepezvineyard@gmail.com

Tastings, tours: June-September, Fri.-Sat. noon-6 p.m., Sun. 2-8 p.m.; October-May, Fri.-Sat. noon-5 p.m., Sun. 2-6 p.m. Free.
Varieties: Blanc du Bois, Cabernet Sauvignon, Chardonnay, Lenoir (Black Spanish), Merlot, Sauvignon Blanc, Shiraz, blends, dessert wine.

David and Lena Yepez, with help from family and friends, put down 400 vines in 2005 to grow Blanc du Bois and Black Spanish (Lenoir) grapes.

Later they built an adobe-style winery between their two vineyards to offer indoor and outdoor hospitality, with a covered pavilion, picnic area and kids' playground. In 2010, they added an olive orchard with the goal of producing and selling olive oil.

Live music is promised on Sunday evenings. Yepez hosts private events and offers a variety of private-tasting packages.

Worth stopping for: The Anahuac National Wildlife Refuge lies between Trinity Bay and East Bay (409-267-3337, http://www.fws.gov/southwest/refuges/texas/anahuac/index.html).

Texas Pairings By Mark Card

Wine to food

What to match with varietals and wine styles used by Texas winemakers:

Black Spanish/Cynthiana: Carne asada, beef short ribs, chili.

Blanc du Bois: Fried catfish, fried okra, corn dogs.

Cabernet Franc: Beef-filled chiles rellenos, cheese enchiladas.

Cabernet Sauvignon: Steak, charcoal-grilled burgers, chili.

Carignan: Cheese enchiladas, beans, rabbit loin.

Chardonnay: Seafood enchiladas, shrimp.

Chenin Blanc: *Dry:* Chicken-fried steak, lobster, chicken. *Sweet:* Crawfish étouffée, peach cobbler.

Gewürztraminer: Corn dogs, glazed ham.

Grenache: Chili, venison, barbecued chicken, Tex-Mex enchiladas.

Malbec: Bacon cheeseburgers, rib-eye steak, seared tuna.

Malvasia Bianca: *Dry:* Pasta with garlic and olive oil, salade niçoise, pizza margherita. *Sweet:* Sheep's milk cheeses, fruit pies.

Merlot: Burgers, home-style dishes like roast chicken, meatloaf.

Mourvèdre: Smoked brisket, baby back ribs adovada.

Muscat Canelli/Orange Muscat: Triple-cream cheeses, cheesecake.

Norton: Blue cheeses, Frito pie, chili, steak.

Petite Sirah: Beef tenderloin, lamb, carne asada.

Riesling: *Dry:* Barbecued sausage, chiles rellenos with cheese. *Sweet:* Blackened fish, corn dogs, pulled pork.

Port-style fortified wines: Strong cheeses, chocolate, roasted walnuts, cigars.

Rosé-style wines (dry): Anything from green salads to grilled salmon.

Roussane: Delicate cheeses, crab cakes.

Sangiovese: Classic Tex-Mex enchiladas, pinto beans.

Sauvignon Blanc: Chicken-fried steak, cheese chiles rellenos, grilled fish.

Syrah: Pot roast, pork tenderloin.

Tannat: Venison, bison, grilled steak, darkest of chocolates.

Tempranillo: Cheese enchiladas, chicken-fried steak, seafood gumbo.

Touriga Nacional: Bison, shepherd's pie, beef stew.

Vermentino: Smoked or grilled trout, chilaquiles.

Viognier: Beans and cornbread, crawfish étouffée.

Food to wine

What to sip with some of Texans' favorite foods:

Brisket, smoked: Mourvèdre.

Bison: Cabernet Sauvignon, Tannat, Touriga Nacional.

Burgers: Bordeaux, Cabernet Sauvignon, Merlot, Rhone blends.

Cabrito: Dry rosés, Tempranillo, Grenache.

Catfish: Blanc du Bois.

Chicken, barbecued: Grenache.

Chicken, fried: Sparkling wine, vermentino.

Chiles rellenos: *Cheese:* Sauvignon Blanc, Riesling (dry or sweet), Semillon. *Beef:* Cabernet Franc.

Chili: Black Spanish, Cabernet Sauvignon, Grenache, Norton, Pinot Noir, Shiraz.

Corn dogs: Blanc du Bois, Gewürztraminer, sweet Riesling.

Enchiladas: *Cheese:* Barbera, Carignan. *Classic Tex-Mex:* Grenache, Sangiovese. *Chicken with salsa verde:* Unoaked Chardonnay, Sauvignon Blanc.

Frito pie: Norton, Zinfandel.

Okra, fried: Blanc du Bois.

Oysters, fried: Sauvignon Blanc, unoaked Chardonnay, Blanc du Bois.

Peach cobbler: Orange Muscat/Muscat Canelli, Chenin Blanc (sweet).

Pecan pie: Fortified Muscat, tawny port.

Pinto beans and cornbread: Carignan, Rousanne, Sangiovese, Viognier.

Quail, fried or grilled: Pinot Noir, Cru Beaujolais (Gamay), dry rosé.

Steak: *Chicken-fried:* Chenin Blanc, Pinot Grigio, Sauvignon Blanc, Tempranillo. *Grilled:* Cabernet Sauvignon, Tannat.

Tacos: *Classic Tex-Mex with ground beef:* Malbec, Shiraz, Rhone blends. *Al pastor:* dry Gewürztraminer, Torrontes, Semillon.

Venison: Grenache.

Alphabetical Index of Wineries

Alamosa Wine Cellars (Central) 10
Arché (N-Central)....................................... 68
Barking Rocks Vineyard and Winery
(N-Central).. 69
Bar Z Wines (W Texas)............................. 59
Becker Vineyards (Central)....................... 11
Bell Springs Winery (Central) 15
Bell Mountain Vineyards (Central) 13
Bella Vista Cellars (Central) 14
Bending Branch Winery (Central)............ 16
Bernhardt Winery (SE)............................ 104
The Blue Armadillo Winery (NE)   91
Blue Ostrich Winery & Vineyard
(N-Central).. 70
The Blue Rooster Winery (NE).................. 92
Bluff Dale Vineyards (N-Central)............. 71
Brennan Vineyards (N-Central)................ 72
Bruno & George Winery (SE)................... 105
Brushy Creek Vineyards (N-Central) 73
Calais Winery (N-Central)......................... 73
Cap*Rock Winery (W Texas) 59
Chisholm Trail Winery (Central)............... 18
Christoval Vineyards (W Texas)................ 60
Circle S Vineyards (SE)............................ 106
Collin Oaks Winery (N-Central) 74
Colony Cellars (SE)................................... 107
Comfort Cellars Winery (Central) 18
CrossRoads Winery & Wine Bar
(N-Central).. 75
Cross Timbers Winery (N-Central) 76
Crump Valley Vineyards (NE)................... 93
Darcy's Vineyard (SE) 108
Delaney Vineyards (N-Central) 76
Driftwood Estate Winery (Central) 19
Dry Comal Creek Vineyards and Winery
(Central)... 20
Duchman Family Winery (Central) 21
Enoch's Stomp Vineyard & Winery
(N-Central).. 77
Fairhaven Vineyards (NE)......................... 93
Fall Creek Vineyards (Central)................. 22

FawnCrest Vineyard (Central) 23
Fiesta Vineyard and Winery (Central) 24
501 Winery (W Texas).............................. 61
Flat Creek Estate (Central)....................... 24
4.0 Cellars (Central).................................. 26
Fredericksburg Winery (Central).............. 27
Fuqua Winery (N-Central) 78
Georgetown Winery and Vineyard
(Central)... 27
Grape Creek Vineyards (Central) 28
Grayson Hills Winery (N-Central) 79
Haak Vineyards & Winery (SE)................ 108
Hilmy Cellars (Central) 30
Homestead Winery (NE, N-Central)......... 94
Inwood Estates Vineyards (N-Central) 80
Kerrville Hills Winery (Central) 31
Kiepersol Estates Vineyards & Winery (NE).... 95
La Buena Vida Vineyards (N-Central) 81
La Cruz de Comal Wines (Central) 32
Landon Winery (N-Central)...................... 81
LightCatcher Winery & Bistro (N-Central)...82
Llano Estacado Winery (W Texas)............ 62
Lone Oak Vineyards (N-Central).............. 83
Lone Star Wine Cellars (N-Central) 87, 88
Los Pinos Ranch Vineyards (NE).............. 96
Lost Creek Vineyard (Central) 32
Maydelle Country Wines (NE).................. 97
McPherson Cellars (W Texas) 63
McReynolds Wines (Central).................... 33
Mendelbaum Cellars (Central).................. 34
Mesa Vineyards (W Texas)........................ 64
Messina Hof Winery & Resort (SE) 109
Messina Hof Hill Country (Central)........ 110
Paris Vineyards (NE) 98
Pedernales Cellars (Central) 34
Perissos Vineyard and Winery (Central) ..35
Pheasant Ridge Winery (W Texas)............ 64
Pillar Bluff Vineyards (Central)................ 36
Pilot Knob Vineyard (Central) 37
Piney Woods Country Winery & Wineyards
(SE)... 111

Pleasant Hill Winery (SE) 111
Poteet Country Winery (Central) 38
Rancho Ponte Vineyard (Central) 39
Red Caboose Winery (NE) 99
Red Road Vineyard and Winery (NE) 100
Retreat Hill Winery & Vineyard (SE) 112
Rising Star Vineyards (Central) 40
Rosemary's Vineyard & Winery (SE) 113
Saddlehorn Winery (SE) 114
Salado Creek Winery & Vineyard
(Central) 41
Sandstone Cellars Winery (Central) 42
San Martiño Winery & Vineyards
(N-Central) 84
SantaMaria Cellars (Central) 43
Savannah Winery & Bistro (NE) 100
Seifert Cellars and Wild West Vines
(W Texas) 65
Singing Water Vineyards (Central) 43
Sister Creek Vineyards (Central) 44
Solaro Estate (Central) 45
Spicewood Vineyards (Central) 46
Stone House Vineyard (Central) 47
St. Rose Vineyard and Winery (NE) 101
Sunset Winery (N-Central) 85
Sweet Dreams Winery (NE) 101
Tara Vineyard & Winery (NE) 102
Tehuacana Creek Vineyards and Winery
(Central) 48

Texas Hills Vineyard (Central) 49
Texas Legato (Central) 50
Texas Roads Winery (NE) 103
Texas SouthWind Vineyard and Winery (SE) 114
Texas Star Winery (SE) 115
Texas Vineyard & Smokehaus (NE) 103
Texoma Winery (N-Central) 86
Three Dudes (and a Dog) Winery
(Central) 50
Times Ten Cellars (N-Central) 86
Torre di Pietra (Central) 51
Triple R Ranch & Winery (N-Central) 87
Valley Mills Vineyards (Central) 52
Val Verde Winery (W Texas) 66
Vineyard at Florence (Central) 53
Wales Manor Winery & Vineyard
(N-Central) 88
Wedding Oak Winery (Central) 53
Weinhof Winery (N-Central) 89
Westcave Cellars Winery (Central) 55
White House Winery (SE) 116
Wichita Falls Vineyards & Winery
(N-Central) 90
William Chris Vineyards (Central) 56
Wimberley Valley Wines (Central) 56
Windy Winery (SE) 116
Woodrose Winery (Central) 57
Yepez Vineyard (SE) 117
Zin Valle Vineyards (W Texas) 67

Other **Texas Pocket Guides** from Great Texas Line Press www.greattexasline.com

Big Bend Guide

"Whether spending two days or 10, author Allan Kimball provides the skinny on what to do, what to see, and how to get there."
—*Texas Highways* magazine

Texas Museums of Discovery

"A handy guide to about 150 interesting and sometimes offbeat museums. You will want to keep this in your glove compartment."
— *Bryan-College Station Eagle*

Texas Landmark Cafes

"You'll never go hungry if you pack this book, which covers the state's four major food groups: barbecue, steaks, Tex-Mex and pie."
— *Dallas Morning News*

Texas 107 Best Walks

"I m keeping this one in the car to encourage me to explore some of the places author Allan Kimball describes."
— *San Angelo Standard-Times*